MIRROR IMAGE

MIRROR IMAGE

REFLECTING THE TRAITS OF CHRIST IN EVERYDAY LIFE

Though this book is designed for group study, it is also intended for personal enjoyment and spiritual growth. A leader's guide is available from your local bookstore or your publisher.

EDITED BY

EVERETT LEADINGHAM

Beacon Hill Press of Kansas City
Kansas City, Missouri

Copyright 1998
by Beacon Hill Press of Kansas City

ISBN: 083-411-7223

Printed in the
United States of America

Editor: Everett Leadingham
Assistant Editor: Charlie L. Yourdon
Executive Editor: Randy Cloud
Editorial Committee: Philip Baisley, Ray Barnwell, Randy Cloud, Russ Gunsalus,
Everett Leadingham, Thomas Mayse, Larry Morris, Charlie L. Yourdon

Cover design: Paul Franitza
Cover photo: Westlight

10 9 8 7 6 5 4 3 2 1

Contents

INTRODUCTION

All of the people who have been involved with the production of this book share one important conviction with Christians everywhere—we want to become as Christlike as possible. To do that, we have looked at the aspects of Jesus' life we can emulate. We can be like Jesus in every characteristic but one—only He could be our Savior.

We have attempted in this book to show the essence of Christlikeness by answering two questions. First, what were the essential character qualities that we discover in the life of Jesus as we read of His earthly life in the Gospel accounts? Second, how can we live our lives in ways that follow the life Jesus led?

The chapters in this study book are laid out in a different way than usual Dialog Series books. Every chapter, except the first one, will proceed through five sections meant to help the reader understand 12 characteristics found in the life of Jesus that can shape, motivate, and activate us to become more Christlike.

The first section is called **A Look at the Characteristic.** This is a one-sentence summary of the attribute of Jesus' life that is the focus of the chapter.

The next section, **A Look at Scripture,** lists the scriptural passage to be explored in the chapter. **A Look at Jesus,** the next section, is a revealing exploration of how Jesus acted and responded in the biblical text.

A Look at Life is a discussion of how our present lives intersect with the biblical story. This is the part where we can make choices to live presently as Christ would have us live.

Each chapter concludes with suggested reflection activities called **A Look at Ourselves.** These thoughtful suggestions can be used to help personally apply the truth of the chapter and to prepare for active participation in each discussion session.

It is our prayer that, as we move through this material, we will see Jesus' life through renewed eyes of faith and find our lives more aligned with the Example.

CHAPTER 1

THE WORD BECAME FLESH

by David A. Higle

A Look at the Characteristic
Jesus is our Savior.

A Look at Scripture
Matthew 1:21; Luke 2:11

A Look at Jesus

I was in eighth grade when I heard someone challenge the Incarnation for the first time. Nancy was a real live wire who usually played the class clown. However, on this Sunday before Christmas she fired a sarcastic, penetrating shot right into the heart of the Christmas story. "What's the big deal about God sending His 'only' Son into the world to die on a cross, anyway? He could always snap His fingers and make another one!"

The rest of us simpletons, including our poor teacher, sat there in stunned silence. No one knew what to say.

Oddly enough, Nancy's cutting question has stuck with me all these years. Provocative encounters have that effect. It was my first serious experience with doubt and led to sincere questions about God and God's way of doing things: Why did God have to send His Son? Could Nancy have a point, did it really *cost* God anything to send Jesus? After all, if He is all-powerful, doesn't that imply He could have devised any number of ways to save us from sin?

Surely He could have simply made a sweeping declaration that would have saved us all: "I hereby pronounce you all to be absolved of your sins!" That would have been easier. Why go to all the bother and fuss of coming to us in the form of a baby—of all things? Indeed, these questions go to the heart of one of the most important doctrines of Christianity—the Incarnation, God coming to us in the flesh in the person of Jesus Christ. So why did God come to us in human form? Why did the Incarnation have to take place?

What Is the Incarnation?

The word "incarnation" means "enfleshment" or becoming flesh. In Christianity, it is the doctrine that in the one person of Jesus, there is the union of human nature with the divine nature. This idea was agreed upon only after 125 years of intense debate in the Early Church. Eventually, this discussion culminated in a council the Early Church held at Chalcedon in A.D. 451. There it was stated that in this union the two natures are united in one person but "without confusion . . . division . . . without separation." One person, two natures. One hundred percent human and 100 percent divine.

Thus, the doctrine of the Incarnation carries with it the belief that God the Son assumed human nature but without in any way ceasing to be God, and without sin (see John 1:14-17 and Hebrews 4:14-15). God the Son was made human (became incarnate) by the Holy Spirit and was born of the Virgin Mary. Thus the entire Godhead is involved: Father, Son, and Holy Spirit.

But what about before His birth that first Christmas? Did the Son exist? Yes. Before His birth to Mary, He always *was*, begotten—not made—from eternity with respect to His deity (see John 1:1). Yet, in respect to His humanity, He was born through Mary, impregnated by the Holy Spirit. The result was not God changing His very nature into that of a human nature. Rather, it was the combining of both the divine nature and the human nature into one living person, Jesus Christ. Two natures, one person. It is vital to uphold this notion as we shall see. This has always been the teaching of the historic Christian faith.

How Can It Be Explained?

The Early Church went to great lengths to explain how two different natures could be found in one person. It took centuries for the Church, steeped in the Greek culture of logic and debate, to carefully word the doctrine. They did this as a defense against heresy. It was vital to the survival of the faith to uphold the doctrine. However, regarding the mystery of the Incarnation, Martin Luther, the 16th-century Reformer, stated, "Reason stumbles at this. . . . You are to believe, not to know and to understand, until the solution appears on the blessed Day of our redemption."[1] Ultimately, it is a mystery. Indeed, there are more types of knowledge than merely measurable, observable facts.

The Scriptures are nearly silent as to the *how* of the Incarnation. The Gospel accounts merely say that the Holy Spirit came upon Mary and she became pregnant (see Matthew 1:18, 25; Luke 1:34-35). Joseph was not the biological father of Jesus. The Bible does not offer up exact scientific explanations as to *how* such mysteries take place. Rather, the Scriptures focus on the *why* of the Incarnation—God loved us so much that He became one of us. The Scriptures, then, spend more time looking at the *life and works* of Jesus, which clearly testify that He was indeed both human and divine.

Christ Was 100 Percent Human

When we look at Jesus in the Scriptures, we see a human being—just as human as you and me—"being in

---

1. Thomas C. Oden, *The Word of Life, Systematic Theology: Volume Two* (New York: Harper Collins, 1989), 98.

very nature God . . . [yet] being found in appearance as a man" (Philippians 2:6-8). Jesus was born, grew, matured, and developed into adulthood just as we do. He experienced all the processes that humans do. He knew what it was to hunger (see Matthew 4:1-4). He was familiar with the wrenching grief and emotional swirl of losing a loved one (see John 11:33-36). He had to learn obedience as we all do (see Hebrews 5:8). On and on the list goes: He enjoyed eating with friends, felt tired from walking long distances, became thirsty on hot days, and, of course, suffered the physical and emotional pain that came with dying a cruel death. There is no question that Jesus was human.

Jesus Was 100 Percent Divine

The Scriptures also portray the divine nature of Christ. Time after time, the Gospels record Jesus performing miracles that utterly defy human origin. He turned water into wine at the wedding in Cana, made sick people instantly well again, healed those who could not walk, cured blindness, displayed absolute authority over the demonic world, raised dead people back to life, manifested power over the forces of nature, multiplied food to feed huge crowds, saw into the inner, hidden motives of people, and much, much more.

As we read these actions of Jesus and ponder their meaning, we are compelled to ask along with the disciples, "Who is this?" (Mark 4:41). Who can do these things? He must be more than a mere man.

In fact, in nearly every account of Jesus' extraordinary works, people are challenged to put their faith in Him. All the works of Jesus point beyond the miracles themselves to the One who performs them. Jesus does what only God can do. The miracles of Jesus are a means to an end and not an end in themselves. They are designed to evoke our faith in Him as the Son of God.

More Evidence

These works of Jesus certainly provide evidence for His deity, but there is more. Jesus also forgives sins, a power that can only be ascribed to God. He allows himself to receive the worship and adoration of others, something that from beginning to end in the Bible is reserved strictly for God.

Then there is the testimony of Jesus himself. Jesus, according to the Gospel of John in particular, understood His unity with God to be more than a unity of wills; it was a unity of essence. The Early Church certainly understood Jesus to be more than just a wise prophet or teacher. They attributed divine qualities to Jesus that in the rest of Scripture are reserved for God. A most notable passage is Philippians 2, an early hymn about the nature of Christ recorded by Paul: "*Who, being in very nature God,* did not consider equality with God something to be grasped, but made himself nothing, taking the very nature of a servant, being made in human likeness" (vv. 6-7, emphasis added). The passage goes on to attest that after His willing obedience led Him to die on the Cross, "God exalted him to the highest place and gave him the name that is above every name" so that "every tongue [will] confess that *Jesus Christ is Lord*" (vv. 9, 11, emphasis added).

There are many other passages in the New Testament that make reference to the divine nature of Christ, such as Romans 9:5: "Christ, who is God over all, forever praised!" And in Colossians 1 Paul said of Christ that "all things were created by him and for him. He is before all things, and in him all things hold together. . . . God was pleased to have all his fullness dwell in him" (vv. 16-17, 19). Still, it is in the resurrection of Christ that we find the most profound evidence of His deity.

The Early Church understood His resurrection from the dead to be the crowning achievement and supreme evidence of all His works and personal claims. Paul wrote to the Romans that Jesus "was declared with power to be the

Son of God by his resurrection from the dead" (1:4). Who else but God can conquer death?

Jesus was both human and divine. The Scriptures are consistent in that claim. But why is all this necessary?

Why Did God Choose Incarnation?

As my junior high friend Nancy asked, why couldn't God have done something much simpler and easier? Why didn't God just give us irrefutable proof of His existence so that we would all believe He is there? Why go to all the fuss of an incarnation? There are many possible answers to these questions, but we will discuss just three here.

First, God desired to communicate with us so much that He spoke in body language—He wanted us to *see* what He was like and not just *hear* about Him. Thus, the concern of the Scriptures is not to offer verifiable proof of His existence but to offer us a picture of who God is. God communicates and reveals himself to us in the person of Jesus Christ. This is one reason why John the apostle refers to Jesus as "the Word" of God.

In the late Carl Sagan's novel, *Contact,* a radio signal from deep within the center of our galaxy has been received by astronomers. Dubbed "The Message," its meaning cannot be deciphered, but it nonetheless sets off a firestorm of controversy around the globe. What does it mean? Is it a hoax? Could it be a message from God, or is it a portent of evil? A battle of words rages between evangelists and scientists over The Message's implication for the existence and role of God. Ellie, the lead character of the novel, is the skeptical scientist who discovers the signal and has this to say to the evangelists:

> What I'm saying is, if God wanted to send us a message, and ancient writings were the only way He could think of doing it, He could have done a better job. And He hardly had to confine himself to writings. Why isn't there a monster crucifix orbiting the earth?

Why isn't the surface of the moon covered with the Ten Commandments? Why should God be so clear in the Bible and so obscure in the world? . . . Why don't we see Him with crystal clarity? . . . You've trapped yourself in some sort of fifth-century mania. Since then the Renaissance has happened, the Enlightenment has appeared. Where've you been?[2]

Through the character Ellie, Carl Sagan, the late astronomer and noted atheist, raises the perennial question (and it is a good question): If God *really* wanted to reveal himself, why didn't He make it simple for us, observable to everyone at all times and in all places—measurable, repeatable, logical—so we could all believe and no one would doubt? Why, instead, did He choose to come in the form of a human baby two millennia in the distant past?

The question is more than one of merely believing in the existence of God. If that were the case, an orbiting crucifix may have done the trick. Still, what would an orbiting crucifix tell us about God? Is He kind or cruel? Is He personal or arbitrary? What is His will for us? And what would it tell us about ourselves? What is our destiny and purpose? What kind of people should we be? Where is the meaning for our lives we all so endlessly crave? Merely knowing that God exists is far from adequate. We need more specific knowledge. So God sent His Son, Jesus, to communicate to us who He is.

God does not accommodate us the way we think He should. A scientific, mathematically verifiable proof for God's existence is not what God desired. Rather, God chose to reveal himself to us, and His destiny for our lives as humans, in Jesus the Christ. In the person and works of Jesus, we see who God is and what He is like. We see His total commitment to those in need. In Jesus, we see His compassion for multitudes and individuals. In Him, we

---

2. Carl Sagan, *Contact* (New York: Pocket Books, 1986), 164, 166.

see God's unconditional love for us, His unrelenting pursuit of those who have gone their own way. Paul sums up the meaning of the person and work of Christ when he writes to the Corinthians, "Though he was rich, yet for your sakes he became poor, so that you through his poverty might become rich" (2 Corinthians 8:9).

The problem, then, is not with the Scriptures but with us. We are like Sagan's character Ellie, who only has room for scientific knowledge as she scoffs at the evangelists. We err when we attempt to squeeze the Scriptures and doctrine of the Incarnation into the preconceived mold of empirical science. Indeed, even today the notion of scientific "fact" is under vicious assault by scientists themselves! So what is the scriptural meaning of the Incarnation? If it is not intended to offer us a scientific proof of God's existence, what are we to do with it? This leads us to our second answer.

Second, the Scriptures boldly state that in the person of Jesus, *God has come to us to redeem us from our sins.* God desires that we might enjoy fellowship with Him for all eternity. "For God so loved the world that he gave his one and only Son, that whoever believes in him shall not perish but have eternal life" (John 3:16). This is why God came in the person of Jesus. He came to provide our salvation.

Only the God-Man Jesus could do this. If Jesus were anything less than 100 percent divine, then God has not truly come to us. If Jesus were merely a man, then we may say that Jesus was a noble teacher, an exemplary model of love for us but not worthy of our worship. He would have died a martyr for His own private cause, as so many others have throughout history. Yet, this is the very teaching being put forth by a host of scholars today who, in their strictly scientific, historical approach to Jesus, have stripped Him of His divinity. They have reduced Jesus to being merely a "peasant sage." Yet, this conclusion can only be reached if we deny the authority of Scripture, discount nearly all of what Jesus claimed about himself, and ignore what the first Christians testified concerning Him.

Likewise, if Jesus were not fully divine, then God himself has not visited with us. God would still be remote and out of touch. If Jesus were less than divine, then God cannot identify with us, has not experienced our frailty, and has no firsthand knowledge of our suffering. The idea that Jesus was just a creation of God sent on a mission—something between God and humanity (like an angel, for instance)—would lead us to what the Early Church identified as a dangerous heresy called Arianism. As we have seen, however, the Scriptures affirm the divine nature of Christ. The writer to the Hebrews states clearly that "we have a great high priest who has gone through the heavens, *Jesus the Son of God*. . . . We do not have a high priest who is unable to sympathize with our weaknesses, but we have one who has been tempted in every way, *just as we are*—yet was without sin" (4:14-15, emphasis added).

Earlier, the Hebrews writer affirms, "Since the children have flesh and blood, he too shared in their humanity so that by his death he might destroy him who holds the power of death—that is, the devil. . . . For this reason he had to be made like his brothers in every way, in order that he might become a merciful and faithful high priest . . . and that he might make atonement for the sins of the people" (2:14, 17).

Since He is 100 percent human, Jesus can adequately represent us before God as our Mediator. Since He is 100 percent divine, He is able to forgive our sins and provide for us eternally. As the Hebrews writer puts it, "Because Jesus lives forever, he has a permanent priesthood. Therefore he is able to save completely those who come to God through him, because he always lives to intercede for them. Such a high priest meets our need. . . . He sacrificed for their sins once for all when he offered himself" (7:24-27). If Jesus were not *fully* human and *fully* divine, there would be no salvation for us before God.

Third, in the person of Jesus, *we see what God originally intended for us, as humans, to be*. In Jesus, we see human life as God originally intended it to be. Before the fall of Adam and Eve, we see them living in an open and free relationship with God and with each other. There was mutual trust, transparent communication, meaningful work, and a notable lack of inner conflict of the will. However, the Fall brought an inhumane quality to all relationships. Distrust, suspicion, obstructed communication, and dishonesty characterize human relationships, even our relationship with God. There is a desire to cover up and protect our own self-interests above all others. Even our struggle to relate in a healthy way to our environment has its start in the Garden of Eden.

Still, in Jesus we see a picture of what it means to be truly human. In His person and works, we have a model of how to really live, of how we were originally designed by God to live. In Christ, we see open, free, and honest relationships before God and others restored. In Jesus, we see exemplified the freedom to live according to truth in accordance with love. And in the atoning for our sins by the God-Man, we have more than just a *model* of how to live; we have the way opened for the power of God through the Holy Spirit to *enable us* to live that way.

That is why an orbiting crucifix or a mathematical proof simply will not do. God wants more for us—and from us—than mere intellectual knowledge of His existence. He wants us to fulfill His original and intended design for us. So He came in the person of Jesus to redeem us, to model human life for us, and to empower us for that life. That is what the Incarnation is all about. That is why it is such a vital and nonnegotiable aspect of the Christian faith.

What Should Be Our Response?

While we feebly attempt to wrap our minds around scholarly explanations of *how* God did it, the Scriptures choose, instead, to focus with clarity on *why* God did it. He loves us. He wants us to be united with Him and He with us. In the Incarnation and in accordance with the consistent teaching of the Early Church, God's ultimate goal is for us to be united with Him. God's highest desire is for us to be who we were originally created and intended to be—fully human beings whose sole and undivided desire is to please God. We are *designed* to find our direction and tasks in life as they flow out of our love relationship with God. God, who spared not His own Son for us, deserves nothing less than our full devotion, love, and undying worship. As Philip Yancy puts it, "Jesus embodies the promise of a God who will go to any length to get his family back."[3]

About the author: Rev. David Higle is an ordained minister in The Wesleyan Church. He is a graduate of Houghton College, Asbury Theological Seminary, and Princeton Theological Seminary. He is currently serving as the Academic Dean at the Zarephath Bible Institute in Zarephath, New Jersey.

---

3. Philip Yancey, "Unwrapping Jesus," *Christianity Today,* June 17, 1996, 34.

CHAPTER 2

IMPROVING YOUR ∫ERVE

by Cleta Crisman

A Look at the Characteristic
Jesus was a servant.

A Look at Scripture
John 13:1-17

A Look at Jesus

So Jesus washed the feet of His disciples. To many readers, this passage of Scripture is so familiar that Jesus' astounding behavior has become little more than a nonthreatening example of humility. Even those hearing the story for the first time may not grasp its significance because the setting is so culturally different from contemporary society. Most of us don't wash any feet except our own. And having a servant to perform such a task would not be a particularly appealing idea to either the host or the guest in most homes today.

However, in first-century Jerusalem Jesus' actions truly were astounding to those present. The Master had performed a service that was the duty of a servant—the very lowliest of servants. Imagine inviting your new pastor for dinner and realizing that he or she wasn't just washing up before dinner but was cheerfully cleaning the whole bathroom. How embarrassing! How humbling!

Perhaps those same feelings were flooding Peter's

mind when he vehemently declared that Jesus would *never* wash *his* feet! Jesus was embarrassing them all with His shocking breach of etiquette. A teacher never washed the feet of his students. Disciples might carry the sandals of the master but never the reverse. No, the students sat at the feet of the master, an official position of subordination and deference to the teacher.

In their view, Jesus was humiliating himself and them in the process. There was no servant in the Upper Room to wash the dust off their feet, so they had gone on with the meal. And then, interrupting their supper—as well as a very stimulating dispute where they were about to determine who among the disciples was the greatest—Jesus suddenly got up, stripped to His tunic, and started behaving like a slave!

We don't really know whether Jesus' washing of His disciples' feet was actually in response to the dispute described in Luke 22:24, but it's clear that He was trying to make an important point about greatness in the kingdom of God. It was His last time alone with His dearest friends. Jesus must have been feeling very burdened with the realization that these men would be the ones to carry on the mission He had begun, introducing both a new spiritual kingdom and the physical evidence of His presence in that kingdom—the Church. He had only a few hours left to prepare them for their roles in the immediate future. Yet, grasping at power and position, the disciples revealed their ignorance of Kingdom values. In washing their feet, Jesus could hardly have chosen a more startling and graphic way to demonstrate those values. Played out on the stage of real life, power and position in the kingdom of God became inseparably linked to humility and service to others.

From the beginning of His ministry on earth, Jesus worked to "deprogram" His people from a superficial, law-centered society and guide them toward holiness from the inside out, a grace-centered community. In their culture, "leader" and "servant" were direct opposites. Although the personal quality of humility had been clearly valued by God through their history, it was not often visibly present in the religious leaders of Jesus' time. The prayer of the Pharisee related in Luke 18:11, "God, I thank you that I am not like other men," seemed to typify the false humility demonstrated by those of his class. Position and authority brought the "privilege" of superiority and condescension. Just as ruling was equated with greater personal value, servanthood was an indication of lesser value—often *no* personal value at all. To say that leaders were called to serve would seem as incongruous as expecting a company's chief executive officer to drive an old clunker car while the janitors rode around in limousines. It just didn't make sense.

Yet that was the point! Jesus was faced with the overwhelming challenge of teaching His people a way of life that just didn't make sense at all. It was a topsy-turvy kingdom with beggars coming to fancy banquets, rich folks choosing to give away their possessions to the poor, and people loving and praying for their enemies. A kingdom of individuals giving up rights and freedom for the sake of others. A kingdom like what might have been if humans had not chosen to worship self over their Creator centuries before in that fateful garden. It was, in fact, a kingdom that reflected the character of God. Jesus knew that the only way such a kingdom could become reality was through one person at a time choosing to live life in a radically different way from the surrounding culture. The men around Him at that last supper held the keys to communicating those radically different ways to the thousands who would enter the Kingdom in the future. Through the power of the Holy Spirit and the cooperation of each leader with that power, the person and character of God would be made visible to the world. The Body of Believers would be the vehicle through which God could touch a hurting world with love and hope. However, only through a body freed from selfish ambition and craving for power could God truly communicate His heart. This Kingdom was to be a kingdom of servants with only one Master— and the Master himself a servant of all.

A Look at Life

Jesus' humble action toward His disciples was not primarily for the purpose of reforming social and cultural behavior. If that were true, we would be scrambling to determine whether it is "relevant" to our present culture and, if so, to which behaviors it would relate. Rather, Jesus was, as usual, demonstrating another characteristic of himself—a picture of true holiness, perfect righteousness. Imagine Jesus—God himself—kneeling on the floor, His gentle, loving hands stroking clean the callused, filthy feet of men who really understood very little about Him. God, a servant? God, the One who created the universe, a menial slave? God, who alone has the *right* to be worshiped, the *right* to demand servitude from every living creature, putting himself in the place of one who has no value? What can it mean? What does it mean for you and me?

The apostle Paul writes in Romans 8:29 that it is God's plan that we be conformed to the image of Christ, and then in 2 Corinthians 3:18 he states that it is in beholding the glory of the Lord that we are transformed into His likeness. When He washed His disciples' feet, Jesus' glory was visible in His example of divine servanthood. His glory is visible in the ultimate act of divine servanthood—allowing himself to be shamed by our sin on the Cross so that we would be free. His glory is visible in the heavenly realms as He serves us now, interceding with the Father every moment on our behalf. His glory is always made visible to the believer through the indwelling Holy Spirit, serving by cleansing, guiding, and empowering. Therefore, if we are to be like Christ, we will be loving servants to Him and to others. How kind of Him to give us a picture of what He desired for us to be so that we would know to cooperate with the efforts of His Spirit to produce the quality of servanthood in us.

When we, Christ's people, become like Him, two wonderful things happen. First, the world has a chance to see Him through us. They can only know what He is like through the picture that is drawn for them by the way we live from day to day, and certainly a sacrificial servant's heart is not a quality that society presently seeks to cultivate. The believer who truly serves in a Christlike way presents a stark contrast to the norm. Suddenly the kingdom of God breaks through the facade of earthly values, and Jesus is made visible to those who are willing to see Him.

When a friend of mine gave up an item in her cart to the woman in front of her who had forgotten to get one, the woman was amazed. She couldn't believe that my friend would cheerfully hand her the item when it meant she would have to return to the crowded aisles to replace it for herself. Such a little thing, but Jesus can gently break through the barriers of an unsuspecting heart with His loving hands—through our own—when He can use them to "wash the feet" of others. When we are preoccupied with *our* images, *our* positions of power, *our* rights, we hide the Light from the world and contribute to its darkness. When we resist serving because of our fear of being hurt, we conceal the Physician who has come to heal not only our hurts but the hearts of those who would seek to harm us.

It is in looking out for ourselves that we reveal our ignorance of the second result of becoming like Christ. At one time, in the beginning, the image of God was glorious and complete in the human being. Communion between humans and God was clear and pure. The intimate bond between Creator and His created beings fulfilled the purpose of that creation. Yet when the choice to sin was embraced, that bond was lost and the image marred. From that moment on, humans have struggled with a sense of incompleteness and unfulfillment apart from God. One by one, those who choose to respond to the wooing of God discover again the truth that their wholeness is solely dependent upon union—or *re*union—with Jesus Christ. According to Colossians 2:10, it is in Christ that we are made complete. It is through the gift of new life through His Spirit that we are once again restored to fellowship with our Creator. This restoration, as we have already seen, does not stop with fellowship but pervades our very nature, transforming us into His likeness—into the very creation we were intended to be in the beginning. As we become more and more like Christ, we experience a greater sense of completion and fulfillment. Becoming a Christlike servant is a means by which we are fulfilled, completed, and healed. It is the safest place for us to be and assures us of our place in the kingdom of God.

How do we do this? What does a servant look like in today's world?

In his book *Reflecting the Character of Christ,* Dr. Les Carter introduces the reader to Miguel, a hospital orderly who tended Dr. Carter during the two months he spent there recuperating from an accident. Miguel, a relatively young man in his early 30s, had begun premedical studies in Nicaragua before being forced to flee for political reasons. His dreams of being a doctor in Nicaragua faded into the bleak reality of a lifetime career as an orderly in the United States. The expectation of days spent bringing health to patients by using stethoscopes, scalpels, and diagnostic skills never came true for Miguel. Instead, his tools were bedpans, bath sponges, and ice pitchers.

Miguel was an excellent orderly, but Dr. Carter was impressed more with his heart than with his skills. In spite of great disappointments, the loss of dreams, and major geographic and cultural changes, Miguel had no bitterness. He was content to do what needed doing, wherever he was placed, regardless of status or recognition. And the most amazing part of all was that he didn't just give himself physically to the task, he truly served from the heart. He seemed to find joy in anticipating even the smallest needs of his patients and genuinely gave all of his attention to their care. Miguel's capable and tender care brought healing to Dr. Carter's body; but even more, the orderly's humble spirit of servanthood was a living demonstration of the profoundly loving heart of Christ.*

Few of us are in circumstances just like Miguel's. We are not called to leave our countries and abandon our life plans. Still, the servant's heart that Miguel demonstrated can be just as powerful in our everyday lives. We all experience disappointments and setbacks, surprises that remind us we are not all-powerful and life does not always conform to our desires. We are all confronted with opportunities to make personal sacrifices for the good of others. We often have to choose between the options of responding to a situation with an eye toward our own needs or with an eye toward what is best for another.

Life brings many situations in which we are called to do things for others that will bring us no attention or recognition. Perhaps our actions will even go unnoticed. How can we overcome the magnetic pull of self-centeredness and fear that makes us cringe at such opportunities for service? How do we cultivate habits of service and still avoid the look of a simpleton who seems to wear a visible label of "doormat"? A closer look at Jesus, our Example, will help us here.

The first thing we notice is that Jesus served because serving was His *nature*. It came naturally to Him. Servant-

---

*Les Carter, *Reflecting the Character of Christ* (Nashville: Thomas Nelson, 1995), 19-22.

hood doesn't really come naturally to us, at least in our original, presalvation state. So if it's true, as we discussed earlier, that Jesus through His Spirit is at work transforming us to be like himself, then our best efforts ought to go into nurturing the relationship that allows this to happen. We read in Romans 12:1-2 that God wants us to be "living sacrifices" and He will transform us by renewing our minds. Giving God free access to our thoughts and attitudes is a powerful way to cooperate with that process. We do this through prayer and Scripture meditations, as well as many other spiritual disciplines.

However, our approach need not always be formal. Simply to be in the presence of God is to be changed, even when it seems nobody's talking. Maybe especially at such times. We can be alert for these moments throughout the course of our days. If we ask God to give us a servant's heart and He is allowed to nurture us with truth, the desire to serve others will become more and more evident.

Another observable trait of Jesus is that He served out of *strength.* He knew who He was. His identity was not dependent upon how others saw Him. God was His Source always, and He often withdrew to spend time with His Father. He was strengthened and validated in His dependence on God. He gave His life away for the sake of others, but He never gave others the power to determine who He was.

Have you ever known someone who always had to be on the giving end and seemed to be dependent upon serving? Perhaps there is someone in your church who always insists on taking meals to those who are ill but won't allow such generosity to be returned. Or maybe someone in your office is obsessed with being the one who brings the goodies, stays late, and makes those extra trips to the post office, never allowing anyone else to play that role. These are not examples of healthy service. Healthy servants never *need* to serve as a source of identity. Their desire to serve comes from the strength of knowing who they are in Christ.

Jesus also served from *freedom*, not obligation. Some people feel their only value is in what they can do for others. There is a sense of obligation to please, regardless of the cost. "Doormats" fling themselves at the feet of others in an effort to prove their own value. Unhealthy servants feel valuable only when that value is verified by others' use of what they have to give. In a sense, it is giving love to receive love, giving something of value in order to be declared something of value. They are "priming the pump" for love because they see the source of love to be another person, rather than God, the true and only Source of love.

Jesus served from freedom because He never *needed* anyone else's response to know that He was valuable and loved. His prayer found in John 17 is a beautiful revelation of the love relationship shared by God and His Son. Verse 23 of that same chapter reveals the wonderful truth that God's love toward each of His children is the same as that for His Son. We can only serve from wholeness when we are healed by receiving the love of our Creator. We can be healthy servants when we do so in the freedom of a heart satisfied by God's lavish love, eager to return that love to God through humble service to others.

We also know that Jesus served out of *obedience* to God. His words in John 5:19 tell us that He did only what He saw His Father doing, nothing of His own initiative. He was so identified with His Father's purposes and desires that His actions always served those purposes. He learned obedience through suffering, disciplining His earthly human self to submit to the desires of God alone. We can follow Jesus' example of Christlike servanthood by watching for opportunities to serve, especially in secret where unhealthy identity or value needs will not be indulged. We can resist the temptations toward selfishness, while cultivating a healthy love and respect for the identity and value God has placed in us. We can ask God every day to take us with Him where *He* is going and allow us to serve Him in the arena *He* chooses for us that day.

It might be relinquishing our place in line at the grocery store, sacrificing the "empty nest" years to care for an elderly parent, showing kindness to an annoying committee member or coworker, giving ourselves the glass with the chip in it, or sending money anonymously to someone in need. (What! Give up a tax deduction?) Regardless of how we serve, we can allow Christ to show himself to others through us, doing what *He* longs to do for those around us. What would you give—or give up—to be the hands of Christ today?

A Look at Ourselves

1. Spend time with God, reflecting on who you are because of Him. Ask Him to help you see ways that you might be depending on others for your identity or value.

2. Ask God to help you be more aware of the ways that others serve you, what sacrifices they might be making for your comfort or convenience.

3. Think about people you have contact with that are annoying or difficult for you to be around. Ask God to help you see them through His eyes, and ask Him to show you if there are ways He would like to serve them through you.

4. Ask God to show you one act of service, however small it might be, that you can do anonymously and regularly (daily, weekly, etc.).

5. At the end of each day this week, take a few minutes alone to reflect on the truth that Jesus is presently serving *you*. Imagine Him kneeling before you, washing your feet as He did the disciples' feet, and realize that He is continually washing you with the living water of His Spirit. Let Him wash away any resentments, any prideful

moments, any selfish ambitions—all the dirt and grime of the daily journey—so that you will be free to love and serve as He desires. Rejoice in your freedom, and thank Him for His great love!

About the author: Cleta Crisman lives in Tualatin, Oregon, with her husband and five children. A recorded minister in the Friends Church, she is active in speaking ministries, writing, and teaching as adjunct faculty at George Fox University.

CHAPTER 3

THE UPSIDE-DOWN KINGDOM

by J. K. Warrick

A Look at the Characteristic
Jesus had a Kingdom perspective.

A Look at Scripture
Matthew 5:17-48

A Look at Jesus

When Paul and Silas came to Thessalonica, as recorded in Acts 17, they began to preach in the synagogue of the Jews. After three weeks, many of the Jews believed in Jesus Christ, along with a great number of Greeks and some of the prominent women of the city. The conversion of these people precipitated unbelievably radical changes in the whole community. While in Thessalonica, they stayed at the home of a man named Jason, who, soon after their departure, was arrested, taken to court, and charged with conspiring with Paul and Silas. His accusers said of him and those who kept company with him, "These that have turned the world upside down are come hither also. . . . These all do contrary to the decrees of Caesar, saying that there is another king, one Jesus" (Acts 17:6-7, KJV). What an incredible indictment! The early Christians were literally taking the Roman Empire for Jesus Christ! In the eyes of the unbelieving world they were turning everything upside down. They were "contrary to the decrees of Caesar." They had to be stopped!

We must admit that it has been a long time since anyone we know has become so concerned about the activities of the followers of Jesus Christ. One pastor said a few years ago that the trouble with Christians is that nobody wants to kill them anymore! While that may be an exaggeration, it could well be an indication that we have failed to fully understand what it means to be followers of Jesus Christ.

The first-century reaction was, "Crucify Him!" And they did—crucify Him, that is. All four Gospels bear witness to the fact that the Jewish leaders conspired with the Roman officials to kill Jesus. The Jews wanted Him put to death because they were convinced that He spoke blasphemy by calling himself the Son of God. The Romans were happy to oblige in order to rid themselves of one more revolutionary and to keep peace with the Jewish leadership. Jesus was perceived as a threat to both the Jewish and Roman cultures. Indeed, He was.

It should have been clear from the very beginning that Jesus would present major problems for all existing ways of living. His message was, "Repent, for the kingdom of heaven is near" (Matthew 4:17). In other words, "There is something wrong with the way you are living, and I am bringing an entirely new way of life to you. Be sad about how you have lived, and turn to Me for life!" Jesus was never one to mince words.

Very soon, He took His closest followers up on a mountainside and began to teach them about life in the new Kingdom. No one before or since has ever presented a more radical departure from life as people had come to know it. Jesus called His followers to what many have called a holy madness, a way of living so far removed from the accepted norm that people might think them mad.

In the Sermon on the Mount (chapters 5—7 of Matthew) Jesus set about defining this "upside-down Kingdom." It was raw gospel. There was no effort to make the truth more palatable, no "spoonful of sugar" here. Jesus set the minds and hearts of His followers spinning with one shocking statement after another. Let's reflect on what He said as He might have said it today:

"You can only be blessed in the most unusual and sometimes unblessed ways."

"You better learn to keep even the least important teaching of the law."

"You must be better than the Pharisees."

In an attempt to get them to understand that sin comes from within rather than from outside a person, He went on to say, "In spite of what you have heard, I tell you . . .

"that anger is as bad as murder."

"that looking at a woman and lusting for her is the same thing as having sex with her."

"that divorce is serious business before God."

"that you never take revenge."

"that you are to love even the most unlovable person around you."

"that you have to be careful how you do the good things in your life such as praying, fasting, and giving."

"that you can't love money and God at the same time."

"that you ought not to be so distracted by what is going on around you."

"that God's interests are more important than anything else in life."

"that you better be careful about judging others. It will backfire."

"that God really wants to give us what is good for us."

"that the way to heaven is marked by a very small entrance."

"that you can't get good things from a bad heart."

"that there is only one way of living that will support the weight of life in the real world."

Wow! After hearing His words, the people went away, shaking their heads and saying that they had never heard anyone teach as this Man taught. He said things as if He really meant what He said!

Jesus called people to follow Him in this new Kingdom lifestyle. Eventually He called 12 men to be His disciples and began the task of educating them in what it would mean to live in this "upside-down Kingdom." He finally sent them out into the world to call all the people of all time to follow Him. This is the call we hear today, "Come, follow me" (Matthew 4:19). When the disciples responded to His call, their lives were forever changed. If you and I respond to His call, our lives will likewise change forever.

We can still misunderstand this call of Jesus by injecting our own ideas into what it means. Some of us think Jesus has called us to become respectable citizens and productive workers, but that is only a by-product. Some of us believe that the call of Jesus is for us to make our nation great again and to make Christianity the state religion. Those issues are external to what Jesus calls us to be. He does not call us to particular political agendas, but He calls all of us to live out the reality of His life on a daily basis. Sometimes that can be done through changing the laws of the land. Sometimes that can by done through helping improve the quality of television programming. Yet, Jesus is not impressed that we are doing all the right things. Rather, He is interested in our character—who we are as His followers (which will profoundly affect what we do). He is not so much interested in the morality of the culture at large as He is with our own moral character.

The call to follow Jesus Christ is at once very personal (you and I must make that decision ourselves), and very corporate (faith can only be expressed most deeply and effectively in community with other believers). It is no small thing to enter this "upside-down Kingdom" and take up the teachings of Jesus Christ as a way of life.

A Look at Life

"Be perfect" (Matthew 5:48). Now that is a mouthful! Jesus said it in the same way He might have said, "Have a good day. Oh, by the way, be perfect."

We are blown away by His plain manner of speech. We are so used to phrasing things in a way that makes them hard to understand that when we hear someone speak clearly, it shocks us. We much prefer the "fine print" of a contract to the plain words of truth. Matthew 5:43-48 provides a laboratory in which we can learn what it means to live the radical "Jesus life."

Is there any way to think through everything you have heard in your life? Think of all the nonsense and foolishness you have heard. I once heard that if you take a penny and rub it on a frog and bury it in the ground. . . . Or was it take a frog and rub it on a penny and bury it in the ground? . . . Or was it a nickel and lizard? . . . Or was it . . . ? Well, it all had to do with getting rid of warts. Anyway, I heard something like that once upon a time. Just think of all the things like that you have heard. A whole lot of what we have been told about the real issues of life is as ridiculous as the penny-frog-lizard-wart thing.

Jesus said that we have heard some pretty logical and rational things about getting along in the world. The only problem is that they won't really work. For instance, one thing we have heard is that we ought to get "them" before they get "us." And if not *before* they get us, certainly *after* they get us, we ought to "give 'em what for." (Now, that's something else I have heard all my life!) Just because someone says something does not make it true. (That's profound, isn't it?) Anyway, Jesus said that we have been told lots of wrong things to do.

This is not everything we have heard along the way,

but it represents so much of what we have heard growing up and after we grew up. What little growing up I did, I did in Texas. I know that you will have trouble believing this, but you can hear some pretty amazing things if you grow up in Texas. I believe I remember that Pecos Bill lassoed the Pecos River and did something with it that it did not want to do. I also heard, "Remember the Alamo," and I do remember. Now, if you are honest, you will have to admit that all of us have heard some pretty bizarre things . . .

> about people of another color,
> and people of other cultures,
> and people of other neighborhoods,
> and people of other lands,
> and people of . . . well, *other* people.

So much of what we have heard is not true. That is what Jesus is trying to teach here in these verses in Matthew 5. Somebody told you to love your neighbors and hate your enemies. Well, come on now, that's not so hard to do, you know. Even a tax collector (Republican? Democrat? Texan?) can do that. That is just business as usual. Surely a Christian can do better than that!

As followers of Jesus Christ, we have been called to live in such a way that our lives will make people think of God. Think about it this way: My daddy was a preacher back in the 1940s. He knew quite a few people down in Texas and Oklahoma. When I began to preach a little, folks who knew my daddy would tell me I reminded them of him in one way or another. I always took that as a compliment. I guess I have always been proud to be my daddy's son. When some longtime friend of my daddy would call me to preach for him, I wanted to do as well as I could so my daddy's friend would think I reminded him of my daddy. I guess we all search for some kind of identity and that was probably a part of my search for whoever I am or will become.

Jesus tells us that we ought to behave in such a way that our behavior would remind people of our Heavenly

Father. To do that we will have to take the same attitude God has toward the world. God gives the rain to the good and the bad. Sometimes it even rains on the bad and the crops of the good dry up and blow away. Did you know that when the sun comes up every morning, the wicked see it just as well as the righteous?

What that means is, when we find out that there is somebody who does not appreciate all our fine gifts, graces, and subtleties of personality and that they have been saying things about us that shock us, we ought to just go on and love them anyway. That's just what God would do if He were in our place. In fact, that is just what God did when He sent Jesus Christ into this world. It's the "God-thing" to do.

After I made a particular decision, someone reportedly said, "He'll pay for that!" Obviously this person did not believe I had done the right thing in the matter. This person "graciously" set out to make my life miserable and was quite successful for a while. I was tempted to tell a lot of things I knew about this person to even the playing field. Then I remembered all the things God knew about me, and He was not telling anyone. It hurt like crazy! I shed a lot of tears during that time, but God gave me a love for my "enemy." Today we are good friends. Now, don't go thinking I am such a good or noble person. It's just the "God-thing" to do.

Jesus wants us to behave in such a way that people might say, "You know that reminds me of somebody like . . . well, like God." They will know that we are the sons and daughters of God, because we remind them of Him.

Are you ever surprised when sanctified (holy) people act as if they are really sanctified? Maybe we all get so used to people behaving like everybody else in the world that we forget there are some real children of God running around out there disguised as ordinary people. Ordinary people living in a hometown, paying taxes, buying groceries, pumping gas, playing ball, stopping at red lights, standing in lines, changing diapers, carpooling, getting married, having kids, and, well, you know, just living—but living by the realities of the "upside-down Kingdom." They don't always stand out, because they are so good at being who they are, but they are out there. They are all over the place just doing the thing they are doing the way God might do it if He were present in a physical body today. That is precisely what is meant by living in the upside-down kingdom of God. Just doing it as God might do it.

Here's the big question: Are you and I living like that?

To do so we must take seriously the teachings of Jesus. Paul said it well in Philippians 2:5-8 when he challenged the believers to take to themselves the very mind of Christ. As we open ourselves to the constant presence of the Holy Spirit, He will teach us exactly how God would respond to a particular situation. He will empower us to do the "God-thing" in every situation.

Welcome to the upside-down Kingdom!

A Look at Ourselves

1. Take some time to read over the passage commonly known as the Beatitudes (Matthew 5:3-12). Which of Jesus' statements turn your world "upside-down" the most (that is, change the way you have been taught to think)?

2. How would you restate some of Jesus' ideas (in Matthew 5:3-12) in your own words?

3. What are some of the ways you have seen others reflect godly qualities in their lives?

4. What are some aspects of your life that you feel remind others that God is your Father?

About the author: Rev. J. K. Warrick is senior pastor of College Church of the Nazarene in Olathe, Kansas. He is married, the father of two children, and a graduate of Southern Nazarene University and Trinity College.

CHAPTER 4

HE DID IT ON PURPOSE

by H. Mark Abbott

A Look at the Characteristic
Jesus had a purpose and focus in His life.

A Look at Scripture
Luke 4:42-44; 9:51-62; 19:10

A Look at Jesus

Mission statements are "in" today. Any organization worth its salt, whether secular, commercial, or religious, has its own mission statement. When I go to the grocery store, there above the door in bold letters is its mission statement. The Christian university across the street from me has its mission statement posted in every campus department. The congregation I serve has a mission, or a vision, statement. Many voices encourage us to develop personal mission statements. Recently I asked our church staff members to develop personal mission statements out of which they would state their objectives for the coming year.

We understand the importance of doing things intentionally, purposefully. Yet, some people today portray Jesus as a well-meaning but hapless martyr to a good cause. His death on the Cross was something He was helpless to prevent. Maybe He was a cut above the norm, but not fundamentally different from religious sages and mystics of any age. Did Jesus really do what He did on purpose?

What Jesus did and said was *not* by accident. In fact, there was a definite purpose for Jesus' whole life. That purpose was clearly expressed by His own words, as well as by the character of what He did. We hear Jesus saying, "I must preach the good news of the kingdom of God to the other towns also, because that is *why* I was sent" (Luke 4:43, emphasis added).

The Gospel passages cited above open a window to the *why* of Jesus' ministry. They suggest at least three purposes for what Jesus said and did.

Jesus' purpose was first *to bring us good news about God.*

Jesus' early ministry in Capernaum attracted attention. He spoke in the synagogue with authority. He healed people of their physical and emotional diseases. One evening, after the sun had gone down, "the people brought to Jesus all who had various kinds of sickness, and laying his hands on each one, he healed them" (Luke 4:40). That must have been wonderfully exciting to the Capernaum townspeople. Imagine having a resident healer in their own town. No need for HMOs or health insurance policies for them!

The next day, when Jesus had gone off by himself for quiet prayer, the crowd sought Him out. They wanted the Healer to go to work again. They wanted Jesus constantly at their disposal. However, He said to them, "I must preach the good news of the kingdom of God *to the other towns also,* because that is why I was sent" (Luke 4:43, emphasis added).

To preach is to proclaim good news. The very word "preach" harks back to the ancient town crier, a messenger sent by the ruler to announce good news from the king. Preaching is literally "good-newsing." That's why Jesus came. The purpose that motivated Jesus to leave the glories of heaven and lay aside the majesty of His divine Sonship was to speak and embody good news.

Jesus' purpose was also to bring us good news about what God is like. Jesus is the divine Word made flesh, God moving into our very neighborhood so that we humans could see with our own eyes what God is like. The apostle Paul wrote to the Colossian Christians about Jesus as "the image of the invisible God" (1:15). Paul added, "For God was pleased to have all his fullness dwell in him" (v. 19).

People today sometimes wonder what God is really like. The final answer to that question is, "God is like Jesus." We bring all our ideas about what God is like to Jesus and test them there. What we see of God in Jesus is good news. Jesus came for the express purpose of bringing us humans good news about what God is like.

However, Jesus also came to proclaim good news about what God's kingdom is. According to Mark's account, "Jesus went into Galilee, proclaiming the good news of God" (1:14). The kingdom of God, in Jesus' message, was not a *territory*, such as the United States. It was a *rule*, the reign of a King across human, territorial boundaries. The kingdom of God is the reign of God among men and women. When this Kingdom fully comes, as the Lord's Prayer implies, then the will of God will be done on earth as it is done in heaven. That's good news, for God's kingdom is one of justice, peace, and love for all.

The good news about who God is and about His kingdom on earth is clearly good news about human salvation. A second purpose for Jesus' coming was *to save us by giving His life on our behalf.*

The passage in Luke 9 portrays Jesus as dissatisfied with the relatively unresponsive ministry He was having in His home region of Galilee. Because Jesus had not come *only* to be a messenger but also a Savior, He was drawn to Jerusalem, the place where He would confront the Jewish establishment, the place where there was personal danger for Him, and the place where He would give himself to save men and women. According to Luke, "Jesus resolutely set out for Jerusalem" (v. 51). A lengthy space in the record of all four Gospels is devoted to Jesus' last days in Jerusalem. It was there that Jesus would give himself by dying on behalf of His own people and the people of the world.

Along the way to Jerusalem, there was opposition. Jesus' disciples wanted to eliminate those who stood in His way by a demonstration of power like that of Elijah, the great Old Testament prophet. However, Jesus corrected their fiery spirit, pointing out that "the Son of Man did not come to destroy men's lives but to save them" (Luke 9:56, NKJV). Jesus did not come to smash the opposition and, in so doing, set up a kingdom of human power and dominance over men and women. Jesus came lovingly to give himself on the Cross for the sake even of those who opposed and vilified Him. Jesus came to bring people into His kingdom by changing them from the inside out. That's what salvation is.

Some people today treat the idea of salvation as a kind of "fire escape," a way of staying out of hell. This perspective views the saving work of Jesus as applying to "the sweet by and by," not "the here and now." Over 200 years ago, John Wesley, father of the Methodist movement, stressed that salvation is not just missing hell or going to heaven when we die. Salvation, Wesley believed, is a here and now thing and involves all God does with human beings from start to finish, "from the first dawning of grace in the soul till it is consummated in glory."[1] What Jesus made possible in salvation, Wesley stressed, is therapy for sin's sickness. Jesus himself used the image of a physician healing those who are sick. Those who recognize they are sick and need the Physician's therapy are made well in salvation.

The purpose of Jesus' mission on earth was thus to announce God's good news to us and to offer us the remedy

---

1. *The Complete Works of John Wesley* (AGES Software, 1997), 14:437.

of salvation made possible through His death on the Cross. Jesus came to do something wonderful for us. Salvation is what God does for us, not what we do for ourselves. However, the scriptures noted in this chapter make clear that Jesus' purpose was also to challenge men and women to be involved in what God was doing in the world.

A third purpose for Jesus' coming was *to call us to Kingdom commitment.*

Luke's story describes some who had half a mind to join the "Jesus crusade," but they apparently were only halfhearted in their interest. "I want to join up with You, Jesus, but I have to take care of some other things in my life." To them, Jesus issued a challenge to wholehearted commitment to His kingdom and its purposes. "Follow me" (Luke 9:59), said Jesus to anyone interested in His kingdom. In this, Jesus' call to discipleship both then and now is unique among world religious leaders. When Buddha was about to die, he made it clear that his followers were not so much to remember him as to follow his teachings. Most world religions involve principles or practices that adherents are supposed to follow. By contrast, all the principles and practices of Christianity are wrapped up in Jesus. "I am the way and the truth and the life," said Jesus in John 14:6.

Jesus' challenge to would-be disciples also involved a focus on Jesus' priorities. Jesus didn't mince words about what His priorities were. Even the birds of the air have the security and comfort of their own nests, "but the Son of Man has no place to lay his head" (Luke 9:58). Even family obligations have to take a backseat to being a Kingdom person. Jesus isn't saying we have to be homeless or ignore our families to follow Him. Jesus is saying we have to get our priorities straight. "Seek first [God's] kingdom and his righteousness" (Matthew 6:33), He challenged His first-century disciples and those who would follow Him today.

The final challenge to would-be disciples had to do

with faithfulness to Jesus. Using the familiar image of a farmer, Jesus said, "No one who puts his hand to the plow and looks back is fit for service in the kingdom of God" (Luke 9:62). The call of Jesus to us is not just to start but to continue and finish.

A Look at Life

How does Jesus' purpose for His life and mission translate into the lifestyle of His 21st-century disciples? Do we really have a purpose for our lives? Is there an intentionality about how we live at home, in our neighborhoods and communities, at work and school, and in our church involvement?

I venture to affirm that most of us do have some kind of purpose. What we say and do betrays the motivation of our lives, but is ours an examined purpose? Is ours a purpose that clearly relates to Jesus' purpose for His life and, thus, for our lives? It is incredibly easy in our secular and self-centered culture to have our purpose for life shaped primarily by the world around us.

Christians, whose model is Jesus, are to emulate the Master's sense of purpose. "Your attitude should be the same as that of Christ Jesus," Paul wrote to Philippian Christians (2:5). As Christ reflects the fullness of God, the disciples of Jesus are, at least in ever-increasing degrees, to mirror Jesus. Periodically I ponder the implications of what Paul wrote to the Corinthians in his second letter: "We, who with unveiled faces all reflect the Lord's glory, are being transformed into his likeness with ever-increasing glory" (3:18). Eugene Peterson paraphrases Paul this way: "We are transfigured, . . . our lives gradually becoming brighter and more beautiful as God enters our lives and we become like him" (TM).

That means that we, too, are to be bearers of the good news of God and of God's kingdom. Is it primarily bad news we proclaim—all that's wrong with the world, with our nation, with other people? Or is there about us the persistent optimism of grace? By our lives and by our lips, do we celebrate the wonder of what God has done and desires to do in human lives and human society? Do we point to the possibilities of grace—forgiveness, new life, healing, restoration of right relationships, meaning to life?

If we reflect the purpose of Jesus, we, too, will be people who give ourselves on behalf of others. OK, so we don't get ourselves crucified for the sake of other people. Nevertheless, do we "wash other people's feet" as Jesus did? Do we take up the role of servant, watching out for the interests of others, not just our own? Do we express compassion for those in need?

Contemporary culture is pervasively self-centered. "Me first" is the way we live, whether it's driving on the freeway, finding a place in a crowded parking lot, failing to respond to the needs of the poor and distressed, disagreeing uncivilly, or venting our frustration on someone who isn't at fault but just happens to be there. Years ago at a busy airport counter, I tried to wait patiently as a frustrated clerk attempted to sort out bungled travel arrangements while the computer system was down. As her internal temperature rose, she cursed the computer with increasing vehemence. Finally, she paused and looked at me. "You must be a preacher!" she said.

I might have responded, "I'm just a follower of Jesus, and I'm trying to act like Him." People who act even a little like Jesus stand out in the dog-eat-dog world we live in.

If we reflect the purpose of Jesus in our lives, we also will be those who accept Jesus' call to Kingdom commitment. Radical though it may seem in the light of contemporary values, we follow Jesus, opt for His priorities, and remain faithful to Him.

Sometimes it isn't altogether clear exactly how the radical values of Jesus expressed in the Sermon on the Mount are to be implemented in a society very different from the one in which Jesus lived. How do we live out Jesus' call to nonretaliation, His comments on divorce and remarriage, and His words on adultery of the mind? Christians have differed on the precise application of some of these Kingdom values to contemporary life, but we do not differ on the reality of Jesus' call to be committed to Him and to His kingdom.

Therefore, how do we stick with the purposes of Jesus? For that matter, how do we stick with any purpose or mission? We all know people who have started well but finished badly. A Christ-centered life purpose must be *formed* but then *maintained*. Often the latter is the most difficult. To consistently implement a Christ-centered purpose for our lives, we need the Christian community, which reinforces that purpose and to whom we are accountable for living it out. Christians are members of faith communities. The extent to which we are involved with our community of faith may well be the extent to which we are able to live out the purposes of Jesus. As John Wesley observed, "holy solitaries" or solitary saints are no more consistent with Christian faith than "holy adulterers."[2]

One Friday morning a few years ago, a well-dressed young man came to our church office and asked to speak to the pastor. It turned out that he was an organized crime soldier who had met Christ through the influence of a woman he loved. The night before he had not followed through on a hit job. He couldn't commit the murder he was assigned. That left him vulnerable to reprisal. You don't just resign from "the family." On the run in a city bus, he saw the cross on top of our church's steeple, jumped off the bus, and asked me for help. I wasn't trained for that kind of request at seminary!

Did this mob soldier stumble into our church by accident? Or did Jesus come so that even this kind of person

---

2. Ibid., 6:60.

might know the Good News, might experience salvation, and become a part of a new kind of "family"—God's kingdom and God's family? Jesus came for people such as him.

However, you don't have to be a mobster to be part of Christ's saving purpose. I know a man who never remembers saying no to Jesus. Growing up in a godly family, responding early to the invitation to give his life to Jesus, opening up like a flower to the influence of the Spirit, entering pastoral ministry as a vocation, this man, too, is a part of why Jesus came. I know, for I am that man!

A Look at Ourselves

1. Are we consciously part of what Jesus came to do in this world?

2. Is it our considered intention to be people who bring Good News by life and by lip, by attitude and orientation toward God, life, and others?

3. Do we give our lives for others? Do we extend ourselves to meet others' needs? Do we believe that Jesus came to save any and all who respond to His invitation?

4. Consider these questions personally: Have you accepted Jesus' challenge to Kingdom commitment? Have you reflected specifically on what that kind of commitment means in your personal life?

About the author: Dr. H. Mark Abbott is senior pastor of First Free Methodist Church in Seattle. He grew up on a mission field in India and is a graduate of Indiana Wesleyan University, Asbury Theological Seminary, Canisius College, and Pittsburgh Theological Seminary.

ſPREADIN' THE NEWſ

by Jesse C. Middendorf

A Look at the Characteristic
Jesus came to proclaim the good news
of the kingdom of God.

A Look at Scripture
Matthew 4:17; Luke 4:16-19, 43-44

A Look at Jesus

Galilee? Of all places, why Galilee? There was no rabbinic tradition that the Messiah would begin His work in Galilee, except for an obscure little reference in Isaiah, but what did that matter? Jerusalem would have been more acceptable. "The melting pot" you might call Galilee. The place where the nation interacted with the nations, where light met darkness. This was the place well-known for fomenting rebellion, fostering independence. Both geographically and religiously, Galilee was far from Jerusalem.

Yet the Gospel writers are unanimous in their assertion that the ministry of Jesus began in Galilee (Matthew 4:12; Mark 1:14; Luke 4:14; John 1:43). Only Matthew, however, mentions Isaiah's prophecy that it was indeed Galilee where the Messiah would make himself known. Galilee, part of northernmost Palestine that first fell captive and was carried into exile during the horrible Babylonian Captivity, would be first to experience the return from exile, said Isaiah. However, the way Matthew read his Scriptures (our Old Testament, Isaiah 9:1-2), Jesus filled Isaiah's prophetic outlook full of new meaning. Oh, yes, exile was ended, and Isaiah's description of light as a metaphor for the relief and joy that accompanied their return is appropriate. Still, to Matthew's mind, the light that Jesus brought would be an even greater light than the glory of the return from exile. Isaiah's "mere" historical fulfillment gave way to the greater fulfillment of the One who brought the greater Light, liberating from sin, not merely from political and temporal dominance.

This is what it means to call the message of Jesus gospel or Good News. This is why Jesus was driven to spread the news.

The record of the early preaching of Jesus is filled with references to freedom, liberation, life giving, healing, and hope. This was a message intended to overcome the despair and futility that often characterized the lives of His hearers. His words and deeds were somehow different from the rhetoric and demand of the Pharisees and teachers of the law. The oppressions of legalistic demands were met with His liberating message of forgiveness, healing, and transformation.

Jesus' hearers marveled at the gracious words He spoke. Repeatedly the Gospel writers make reference to the amazement of those who heard Him. His words carried authority, grace, hope. It was in stark contrast to the religious experts who, according to Jesus, loaded people down with "burdens they can hardly carry" (Luke 11:46).

The character of the message of Jesus was made clear in Luke's account of His early ministry at the synagogue in Nazareth (4:16-30). His message on that occasion set the pattern for His life's work. It was to shape the entire narrative of Luke through both the Gospel and the Book of Acts.

As Jesus stood before the synagogue in Nazareth, He read the prophet Isaiah. In doing so, He revealed the true nature of His ministry. Though He was alternately approved and opposed, though the responses to Him throughout His ministry ran the gamut from believing faith to furious opposition, His mission never wavered.

Luke, extending his narrative of the life and work of Jesus throughout the Gospel of Luke and into the Book of Acts, demonstrated consistently how the life, ministry, and message of Jesus coincided. He embodied the words He read from the prophet while in Nazareth, and His ministry "filled full" all the gracious implications of that princely prophet's words.

The words of Jesus were words of hope rather than words of condemnation. Oh, not that He ignored sin or overlooked the necessity of righteous living. Rather, Jesus understood that the mission on which He had embarked was the means by which people *could* live righteously. His was not a message of demand and condemnation to the lost and the failing. It was a message of hope and possibility for a people who feared never being acceptable to God because of their utter inability to fulfill the requirements of the law on their own.

Nor did Jesus overlook the hardened, exclusive spirit of religious zealots who had become so blinded to the true nature of God that they increasingly opposed the gracious message of Jesus. Throughout His ministry, Jesus' message was the same: "God's inclusive kingdom is here. Turn around and get on board!"

The message of Jesus was not limited to the familiar environment of Galilee. He crisscrossed all of the land, His journeys taking Him from the far north at Sidon on the shores of the Mediterranean to the religious heart of Judaism at Jerusalem.

Nor was this message limited to the Jews alone. Throughout His ministry, Jesus was thrown into contact with those from outside the Jewish nation. His beginning ministry in Galilee ("the melting pot"), His reference to Elisha's ministry to Naaman the Syrian (Luke 4:24-27), His ministry to the Samaritan woman (John 4:1-42), His response to the Greeks at the feast in Jerusalem (John 12:20-26), the Great Commission (Matthew 28:19-20; Acts 1:7-8)—all these were indications that His mission was to fulfill God's purpose to form a people of all nations.

Not everyone understood or appreciated His message. The reaction of the people of His hometown was vicious and threatening. While many in other places gladly received Him and believed His message, there was a growing effort by religious and political leaders to thwart His ministry, eventually to do away with Him altogether.

What remarkable tenacity Jesus demonstrated! What unwavering focus! Throughout His ministry, He continued His passionate appeal to the lost and wandering ones, even when the religious leaders misunderstood Him, opposed Him, and sought to kill Him. He was so driven to fulfill His mission that nothing could deter Him. When the religious establishment accused Him of socializing with the dregs of society, He readily acknowledged it, claiming His responsibility to bring news of the inbreaking kingdom of God to "the lost sheep of Israel" (Matthew 15:24) or to "the sick" (Luke 5:31). However, even among the establishment there were those who heard Him, believed Him, and put their faith in Him (John 12:42).

When approaching Jerusalem near the end of His ministry, knowing the magnitude of the final conflict that lay ahead, He wept over the city with compassion and heartbreak. Never vindictive toward His accusers or short of patience with those who resisted Him, He poured out His heart in love, appealing to them with the depths of His concern. Yet whenever He spoke, there was a ring of eternity in His words. The issue was not His popularity or their approval. The issue was redemption. The concern was for their souls.

It was for that reason that so much of His message

sounded like judgment. His opening words of invitation were, "Repent!" (Mark 1:15). This was not the railing of a frustrated prophet. This was the fervent appeal of the Redeemer-Man, who knew the consequences they faced for failing to heed His words. This admonition was direct and impassioned, but perhaps less harsh and demanding than it sounds to our ears. His words should perhaps be understood to mean, "Turn your lives around, because here comes the kingdom of heaven."[1] His words were identical to those earlier used by His forerunner, John the Baptist. The basic meaning of the word we translate "repent" could mean "turn around" or "change." This is not a hard word to understand, not one that requires extensive explanation or definition. It means simply that whatever preoccupies our thinking, or that would hinder our fully turning toward God, is that from which we should turn. It is much more than merely a change of mind or regret. It is a complete change of direction. And this change in direction is enabled by the very word spoken by Jesus.

The further words of the message, "The kingdom of God is near" (Mark 1:15) have been suggested by one writer to better read, "Here comes the kingdom."

> These words announce a *fait accompli** and could suggest that there is not much we can do about it. But when Jesus attaches to His [message] the word "turn around," Jesus honors us. He helps us, telling us there is something we can do about it; indeed, that there is something we must do. . . . When Jesus here says "turn around," He releases with that Word—even to us who hear that Word today—the spiritual power to turn around or the power to ask for power to turn around.[2]

---

1. Frederick Dale Bruner, *The Christbook,* vol. 1 of *Matthew* (Dallas: Word Publishing, 1987), 119.

*Fait accompli: a thing accomplished and apparently irreversible.

2. Ibid., 121.

It was this dimension of His message that was so dynamically different from the demands of those Pharisees who saw no grace in the law. It was this that caused so many to find His words to be life and bread. No wonder it is called gospel or Good News. This is world shaking! This is hope-filled! This is transforming!

But this is also confronting. The appeal to Judaism was consistent, focused. While there were others who were given opportunity, Jesus spent most of His time appealing to His own people, the Jews. Their resistance, growing opposition, and eventual bitterness were not merely ignored. Jesus met their antagonism, not with bitter reaction, but with stern warning. While He spoke with healing to those who responded to His message, He was abrupt and forceful in His attention to those who had so hardened their hearts that they could no longer hear the Father speaking through Him.

Yet throughout His ministry, the words of the prophet Isaiah continued to define His mission. The blind were given sight. The lame were made whole. The oppressed were liberated through forgiveness. This was indeed "the year of the Lord's favor" (Luke 4:19).

A Look at Life

If this *is* the message of Jesus, the world is hungry to hear it! This word needs to be spread. The insistent, persistent ministry of Jesus, even in the face of opposition and threat, sets the agenda for His followers. The timid, self-obsessed focus of some Christians finds itself confronted by the blazing eyes of the Redeemer, who, with words too bold to be ignored, walked courageously through the land, even into the Temple itself, and called men and women to repentance. The force of His words might better be understood if we hear them like this:

Move! Here comes the whole new world of God! Almost every word is nuclear. This thematic sentence tells us that we had better change *now*, get out of the way *now*—or, more precisely, get *in* the way now—because in Jesus' Word, God's mighty new world is on its way toward us and is even now crashing in. "Change! Here it comes!" This is the sense of the expression."[3]

Let me illustrate one way this message gets spread. Darryl and Verna Stanton were preparing for the mission field, and they were growing in anticipation of their departure for Africa. However, they were also keenly aware of their neighbors in the apartment complex. One of them, a young single mother, was struggling with the demands of raising twin daughters alone, having just come through a difficult and draining divorce. Darryl, Verna, and their children became acquainted with the three of them, often inviting them to their home and assisting the young mother with her growing and active young daughters.

Not content to merely befriend their new acquaintances, the Stantons often shared their faith. Though quiet and shy themselves, they felt the urgency of inviting Sandy and her daughters to join them in church activities and of frequently talking to them about spiritual things. Darryl and Verna were never critical, never judgmental. Still, their assurance of God's love and the conviction of the necessity of knowing Christ as Savior had an impact. To Sandy, it was as if they knew of a whole new world of realities of which she was totally unaware!

One evening Sandy accompanied them to a church drama presentation. A student of speech and drama herself, Sandy was completing her master's degree and was preparing to teach in a local college. Sandy had been struck by the love and friendliness of the Stantons and discovered a church that seemed also to be oriented to realities she did not know existed. Stirred and impressed by the love of the church, Sandy opened her home to a team of visitors from the church and soon opened her heart to the Savior. Not

---

3. Ibid., 123

long after, her young daughters also gave themselves to Jesus. Now, several years later, the grown daughters—soon to graduate from a Christian college—and their mother are active leaders in the life of that very church. They consistently share their faith with others with an urgent simplicity that invites them to discover the best news of all: "Turn around! Here comes the kingdom of God!"

This is news too good to be kept to ourselves. It is impossible to hear these words with the force with which Jesus intended them and not be affected. The words that fell from the lips of Jesus in the synagogue in Nazareth, though gracious, were also stunning. The hearers were confronted with a necessity. They had to respond!

And you? What will you do? When you hear these words, really hear them, what will you do?

A Look at Ourselves

1. Review Luke 4:14-30. What characterizes the message and ministry of Jesus? What words would you use to describe what He said in Nazareth?

2. Compare the message of Jesus in Nazareth to the parables of Jesus in Luke 15. How does this alter your understanding of His message?

3. What connection do you see between Luke 4:14-30 and Luke 5:27-32? To whom do you think Jesus might expect you to go?

4. What priority do you think Jesus would expect you to place on helping others to know Him? (Matthew 28:18-20; Acts 1:3-8)

5. How might you encourage one another in your group or church to become involved in "spreadin' the news"?

About the author: Dr. Jesse Middendorf is senior pastor of First Church of the Nazarene, Kansas City.

Chapter 6

Jesus Loved Them All

by Rebecca Laird

A Look at the Characteristic
Jesus loved sinners.

A Look at Scripture
Luke 19:1-10

A Look at Jesus

On His way from Galilee to Jerusalem, Jesus stopped in Jericho, the ancient "city of palms," centrally located in the fertile Jordan Valley. Jericho's markets teemed with fresh produce and fine goods, which made the city a crossroads for traders and travelers. In planning an itinerary in first-century Palestine, Jericho would rank as an appropriate place for Jesus to rest up and restock after a long journey through dusty, poor villages where the sick, the possessed, and the dispossessed flocked to Him. Jesus knew that the next leg of His journey would be arduous. The road from Jericho to Jerusalem was the same treacherous setting of the story He had recently told of a man beaten by robbers and left to die. Only the kindness of a stranger, the good Samaritan, had saved the man's life. The Jericho Road and Jerusalem—the place of Jesus' triumphal entry and agonizing crucifixion—awaited Him on this journey.

However, in this in-between time, as Jesus approached Jericho, a blind man called out, begging for his sight to be restored. Jesus stopped, listened, and healed him, crediting the man's newfound sight to his faith. The news spread fast. Crowds gathered to see the itinerant Teacher who had been raising questions and hopes throughout the surrounding area.

Zacchaeus, Jericho's chief tax collector, wanted to see Jesus too. It should be no surprise that Zacchaeus climbed to such heights to see Jesus. After all, what tax collector wouldn't want to see the Preacher who had recently and publicly told a parable about a publican and a Pharisee who went to the Temple to pray? In fact, in this parable Jesus praised the publican for the humility of his prayers!

Even earlier in Galilee, Jesus had called a tax collector named Levi to be one of His disciples. Levi had thrown a big banquet for Jesus and invited his fellow tax collectors to dine with his new Master. We don't know if Zacchaeus might have been among them. Yet, it is certainly possible that word of this Teacher who was a friend to tax collectors had passed among the members of this profession. What we do know is that the Pharisees and teachers of the law complained about Jesus' choice of friends to His disciples: "Why does your teacher eat with tax collectors and 'sinners'?" (Matthew 9:11).

Why, indeed, did the Son of God, the Holy One of Israel, eat, drink, and spend time with people like this? Why didn't He steer clear of tax collectors like all the other self-respecting, law-abiding rabbis? What was Jesus doing? Anyone who would speak well of a tax collector in first-century Palestine would garner negative public attention. Tax collectors weren't duly elected officials or public servants. They were enterprising, already wealthy citizens who bid on the chance to collect taxes for the Roman Empire. The top bidder was awarded the contract and the power to exact taxes from local farmers when they sold their goods and from traders who carried these goods over local borders to distant markets. For providing this service to the Empire, the tax collector could levy an additional fee, which he often set himself, as his own compensation. In addition, since many of the taxes were paid with a portion of the goods, the publican could turn around and resell the grains or goods at marked-up prices, further increasing his profits. When a farmer couldn't pay the tax, publicans often loaned the money at exorbitant interest rates, and when the loans weren't repaid, the farmer's land was repossessed. By contemporary standards, a tax collector could be guilty of loansharking, extortion, double-dipping, and racketeering for simply doing his job well. It's no wonder tax collectors were a despised group!

Jesus wasn't going to be around for long; He was just passing through. So what was a short guy such as Zacchaeus to do if he wanted to see this Healer and Teacher with his own eyes? He knew no one would give him a chance to muscle to the front row for a good view. The crowd was likely to link arms and bar him completely, for they had so few opportunities for revenge against tax collectors like him. If he stood in the crowd, he would give the many who despised him ample opportunity to get in an anonymous kick or push. Zacchaeus could hardly pass unknown in any crowd. He must have been well-known for being on the scene to tax farmers who tried to move their goods to market and to collect taxes from the market vendors once they set up their booths. Every time someone tried to make some money, there he was with his hand out to take the government's share and an extra measure for himself.

Zacchaeus, being the clever sort, finagled a good viewing spot for himself. As Jesus passed by, He looked up, saw Zacchaeus, and invited himself over for food, drink, and rest. Wherever Jesus went, His entourage of disciples and followers went as well. Zacchaeus welcomed them gladly.

However, the crowds began to rumble. They always do when a bad guy gets put front and center. Why was Jesus paying attention to this arrogant cheat? It feels so good to see a public sinner get sentenced for doing wrong. When a slimy, stealing cheat gets the attention and gets forgiveness as well, it upsets our sense of justice. It's not right for a robbing braggart such as Zaccheus to get to spend hours talking to Jesus. If Jesus had singled out a widow and her hungry children, He would have proven that He was firmly on the side of the poor. Instead He picked one of the most despised men in town. Why did Jesus pick him?

Why indeed? It's no mystery. Jesus answered His critics in Jericho much as He had His critics in Galilee, who had wondered why He ate and drank with sinners. He said, "Today salvation has come to this house, because this man, too, is a son of Abraham. For the Son of Man came to seek and to save what was lost" (Luke 19:9-10). Those who wanted Jesus to punish this man for his greed heard a word of grace instead.

By His words and actions, Jesus gave Zaccheus a new identity. Rather than being a despised, greedy, good-for-nothing outsider, Zaccheus was publicly proclaimed by Jesus as an insider in God's society. He was a "son of Abraham," an inheritor of God's promises. In Luke 3:34, Jesus' genealogy shows that by birth, Jesus is a son of Abraham. So by calling Zaccheus by this title, He was, in essence, calling him kin. To be sure, Zaccheus hadn't earned his place in God's family, but then none of us do. Jesus called out to Zaccheus, and he responded, welcoming Jesus into his heart, home, and bank account. That is what makes us members of God's family as well.

Jesus understood that Zaccheus was lost, that he had lost track of himself as a member of God's family. According to William Barclay, to be "lost" in the New Testament use of the word means "to be in the wrong place."[1] Rather

----

1. William Barclay, *The Gospel of Luke* (Philadelphia: The Westminster Press, 1975), 235.

than decreeing that Zacchaeus was doomed or damned, which only God decides, Jesus showed us that Zacchaeus needed to be returned to the place that was his to occupy. He, like all of us—1st-century and 21st-century people alike—had a graciously offered place to occupy in God's family.

The Bible speaks often about the poor and the down-and-out, making the clear point that God cares about the poor and oppressed. The basic needs of people need to be met. God's good creation offers the resources to meet everyone's needs but not everyone's greed. Knowing this, we'd expect Jesus to take all from Zacchaeus and give it to the poor—like a divine Robin Hood. Instead, Jesus welcomed Zacchaeus into His brotherly embrace. That love, acceptance, and forgiveness brought Zacchaeus back into a right relationship with God.

What happens when the lost are found? If Zacchaeus is any indication, we see that when we are found, included, and aware of our identity as God's own, we give ourselves away in acts of radical self-giving. Zacchaeus went beyond the law in collecting taxes and enriching himself, and he went beyond the letter of the law in making restitution. He said to Jesus in a statement of giving and restitution, "Look, Lord! Here and now I give half of my possessions to the poor, and if I have cheated anybody out of anything, I will pay back four times the amount" (Luke 19:8).

He didn't make this offer privately, either. He made it there in front of God and everyone. Those teachers of the law, present when he made his restitution, knew that he was going beyond the requirements of the law. The penalty for deliberate stealing and destruction of property according to Exodus 22 was double repayment (vv. 4 and 7). In Numbers, anyone who wrongs another must confess, make full restitution, and pay one-fifth more (5:7). Any judge in Israel would have probably been easier on Zacchaeus than his own conscience was. Jesus' friendship meant so much to him that he was willing to give what he'd worked so long and fiercely to gain. Jesus' approval and companionship was worth more than any amount of money or power. It still is.

A Look at Life

Zacchaeus's story raises several very important life questions: Why does Jesus love everybody, including greedy tax collectors and the people we can't stand—all those that think, dress, and believe differently than we do? And how does He do it? Let's briefly look at each of those questions.

Why does Jesus love everybody, including people like Zacchaeus, who have done grievous wrongs to the innocent? If Jesus doesn't judge others by our standards, what standards does He use?

If we read through the Gospel of Luke, we begin to see a pattern of regard Jesus had for others. Jesus knew that each and every human being is created in the image of God. No one—not the immoral, the imperfect, nor those impervious to God's Spirit—is without the divine spark that faith fans into full flame. Genesis tells us that we bear the holy mark of God's design in our very beings, whether we acknowledge it or not. God sees us all as beloved children.

Mother Teresa of Calcutta was a modern model of how viewing others as bearers of God's image transforms our ways of relating to each other. She described one of the many dying, destitute persons she picked up from the streets and cared for in this way: "That man, so smelly, so disfigured, is my brother, the image of God."[2] When she

---

2. This is a quote from a taped conversation Mother Teresa had with Michael Christensen in Calcutta in August 1984. Mother Teresa was famous for saying the same thing, in essentially the same way, a thousand times.

came in contact with a sad soul, she didn't accept the label of untouchable that was given by society; instead, she saw each person as a bearer of God's own image. She also understood that "the worst poverty in human life is not for bread or rice, but to be loved. . . . The worst disease in the world is not leprosy or tuberculosis but the feeling of being unwanted, unloved, and abandoned by everyone."[3] To be lost, like Zacchaeus, is to consider oneself outside of God's care and beyond the reaches of human love. Mother Teresa simply followed the way of Jesus. She did in Calcutta what Jesus did that day in Jericho when He declared that Zacchaeus, a man despised by many, was a "son of Abraham," an insider in God's family.

When we look to Scripture, we can begin to see how Jesus loved everybody. The most essential ingredient to Jesus' openness toward those He met was being rooted in God's ways. Throughout the Gospels, we see Jesus was steeped in Scripture, and He regularly sought out solitary places where He prayed, seeking God's peace and guidance. When He knew what God would have Him do and be, He returned to the villages filled with people who had innumerable needs. Because Jesus followed a rhythm of prayer and action, He knew who to heal, who to heed, and when to move on. No doubt His spiritual sensitivity to God's Spirit was what drew Him to Zacchaeus, not the fact that this little guy had the nerve to climb a tree. When we are well-rooted and frequently watered by the wellsprings of Scripture and prayer, we, too, can be led by God's Spirit to reach out and allow ourselves to be channels of God's love, hope, and healing.

Once we are led by God to reach out to another, Jesus' example shows us what to do. First with the blind beggar on the road to Jericho and then with Zacchaeus, Jesus be-

---

3. Georges Gorree and Jean Barbier, eds., *The Love of Christ: Spiritual Counsels, Mother Teresa of Calcutta* (San Francisco: Harper, 1982), 26.

gan by stopping to look directly at the person's situation. He gave up His itinerary and put the person top on His priority list. So first, when we want to be available to others, we have to stop, give up our agenda, and be present to another person. Then Jesus spoke directly to the person. To the beggar He posed a question: "What do you want me to do for you?" (Luke 18:41). To Zacchaeus, He gave a command: "Come down immediately. I must stay at your house today" (19:5). In both instances, He related to each one as a person to be known, not a problem to be solved. The blind beggar had great faith, and Jesus recognized it. Zacchaeus had great material resources, and Jesus drew upon them. Both the beggar and Zacchaeus gave extravagantly of what they had out of gratitude for Jesus' personal care and transforming love.

We must never underestimate the power that comes from treating another with dignity, compassion, and honesty that springs from our love for God. One of the priests who worked with Mother Teresa tells the story of a leper who tried to use his disfigurement for personal gain. One evening when he saw some ladies alone, he approached and demanded money. He threatened, "Give me money, or I will touch your faces, and you will be lepers." In fear, the women did what he asked.

When the priest heard of the leper's actions, he sought him out and offered a stern reprimand. The leper showed no remorse until the priest yelled at him, "Yes or no, are you a man?"

At this the leper stood and said, "You are right; I did wrong. I am a man." Because he had been treated as a person, not a disease, he added, "Thanks." A call to his humanity quickened his sense of right and wrong.[4]

To treat persons as creations of God, to love insiders in the family of faith—even before they know themselves to

---

4. Ibid., 36.

be such—is to love as Jesus loved. We are often tempted to draw circles to define who is an insider and who is an outsider in God's family. Jesus shows us that instead of drawing circles of exclusion, we are to reach out person-to-person, day by day. As we listen, learn, and share of the love and truth God has given us, we will discover that God has an infinite capacity to add more branches to our shared family tree.

A Look at Ourselves

1. Here is an exercise to help identify the "tax collectors" in your life:

This week pay attention to the news stories or local events that raise your hackles. Does a particular person or group of people engaged in certain beliefs or behaviors make you angry or spiteful?

Perhaps someone has taken advantage of you for personal gain. Imagine Jesus coming to your town and inviting himself over to the home of one you can't tolerate. How would you respond?

As one of Jesus' disciples, would you follow Jesus to a place where you would not go on your own? Can you pray for a person you dislike?

Make it a priority to include such a person or group in your prayer list this week. If your paths cross, say something, even if it is simply "hello." Remember, too, this is a person to be known, not a problem to be solved.

2. Here is a journaling question:

When Jesus came to Zacchaeus's house, Zacchaeus welcomed Him and began to return all of the things that he wrongly took from others. Write in your journal, then answer this question: Jesus is coming to my house today. Will Jesus find anything here that doesn't belong to me? Will He find anything that keeps me from loving others as I should? What must I do to prepare my home and heart to freely welcome Jesus?

3. An act of gratitude:

This week do something extravagant out of gratitude for the friendship you have with Jesus. Send an extra check to your favorite charity. Or better yet, volunteer a few hours. Order flowers for your pastor or Sunday School teacher. Offer to rake a neighbor's leaves or to carry up groceries from the apartment landing. Find a way to give yourself to others.

About the author: Rebecca Laird, an ordained minister, is a staff consultant to The Lamb's Church of the Nazarene (Manhattan, New York). She is the editor of *Sacred Theology: The Journal of Fellowship in Prayer.*

CHAPTER 7

LOVING THE ONES WHO HURT

by Patty L. Craft

A Look at the Characteristic
Jesus had compassion.

A Look at Scripture
Matthew 15:29-39

A Look at Jesus

Jesus spent the majority of His short time here on earth teaching His 12 disciples a lifestyle of compassion. After His death, it would be their responsibility to continue the message He brought. His lessons came through a variety of methods. He used sermons, casual talks as they worked, and private conversations to communicate God to them. However, the most effective were probably the visual, hands-on lessons.

The miracle feeding found in Matthew 15:29-39 is one of these lessons. The importance of this miracle can be seen from the fact that the compassionate feeding of a large crowd is recorded in every Gospel. The retelling in Mark 6 shows Jesus and His disciples weary from the demands of the crowds that were coming to them. They entered a boat to get some rest for themselves. Yet, as they arrived on the other shore, the crowds were there to meet them.

Jesus' reaction was not annoyance at the missed opportunity of rest. Jesus' life was people-centered. A person or crowd in need always filled His heart with compassion. Jesus wanted to teach this same reaction to His disciples. His compassion would be both their example and motivation in order to fulfill Jesus' call on their lives.

Throughout the Gospels Jesus sought to minister to the needs of all people with genuine love. This complete picture is revealed in the "I am" statements found throughout the Book of John. Expressed in symbols familiar to the people during His time, these declarations reveal the relationship Jesus has to our spiritual needs and the compassion He had for all people.

In the statement "I am the bread of life" (John 6:35, 48), bread represents the satisfaction Jesus gives for our desire for life. In John 8:12, "I am the light of the world" refers to Jesus being the Source by which we can distinguish truth from falsehood.

The often-used analogy of Jesus being a shepherd is found in John 10:7. "I am the gate for the sheep" refers to the shepherd's duties to the sheep. At day's end, the shepherd stood at the doorway, counting and checking each sheep. He anointed wounds with oil, and he distributed water. After all entered the pen safely, the shepherd kept watch at the gate, protecting the defenseless sheep from any harm during the night. This is a perfect picture of Jesus as our Guide and Protector in life.

John 14:6 sums up these and the other "I am" statements with a simple foundation for life. Not merely does Jesus *know* the way and truth, but He *is* the Way and the Truth—the answer to our problems. A relationship with Jesus is the life we seek. All of these "I am" statements refer back to the compassion Jesus feels for everyone.

Compassion is one of the lessons that must always be learned by doing. No one can truly understand compassion by reading a book about it or taking a class. It is a hands-on lesson that must be experienced to be truly learned.

A key factor in Jesus' compassion was His availability. Jesus was never so preoccupied with His mission that He ignored hurting people. Matthew 20:28 reminds us that "the Son of Man did not come to be served, but to serve, and to give his life as a ransom for many." He was never so overscheduled with His destiny to ignore needy people. Some would say He put aside His own agenda, when, in fact, bringing God to people was His agenda. He was daily fulfilling the greatest commandment He gave to the disciples: "'Love the Lord your God with all your heart and with all your soul and with all your mind.' This is the first and greatest commandment. And the second is like it: 'Love your neighbor as yourself'" (22:37-39).

Jesus used these acts of compassion to answer questions about His messianic role. Imprisoned and near the end of his life, John the Baptist sought reassurance from Jesus. John sent his disciples with one simple question: "Are you the one who was to come, or should we expect someone else?" (Luke 7:19).

The answer to this question was found in Jesus' actions. He divided it into two simple categories—physical infirmities were healed and good news was preached to the poor. Compassion was His calling card. Yes, He was the One to come. He had fulfilled the Old Testament's predictions of how to recognize the Messiah (see Isaiah 29:18-21; 35:5-6; 61:1).

Throughout the New Testament, we are introduced to the compassionate Christ. On a daily basis, Jesus took responsibility for the people who came across His path. Most of the people Jesus helped were not friends or relatives.

He did not spend time deciding who deserved help and who didn't. Skin color, religious background, gender, economic status, or age was irrelevant. He looked beyond the exterior to the interior. Because Christ's compassion did not measure worth as the world did, He seemed to minister indiscriminately. He saw problems as opportunities. Simply put—He saw, He felt, He responded.

Jesus demonstrated what one Christian writer calls true service. True service delights in serving. It is not concerned about results as self-righteous service is. Self-righteous service wants to make sure people see and appreciate its good work. We are still in charge in self-righteous service. We decide how and when serving will fit into our schedules.[1]

This is especially prevalent at Thanksgiving and Christmastime. There is no end to the volunteers available to charitable organizations when some self-righteous servers want to feel good about their service. True service means being a servant. It means giving up the right to be in charge. True service is a lifestyle, not a scheduled event.

A Look at Life

Our first step toward Christlike compassion, or true service, is opening our hearts to God. A cartoon I have posted above my desk challenges me daily. The first character says, "I often want to ask God why He allows poverty, hunger, and injustice in the world." The second character responds, "Why don't you?" Then the first character confesses, "I'm afraid He will ask me the same thing." As is often the case, the questions I pose to God are handed back to me.

If we let God fill us with compassion, we, too, will be moved to action—not moved to serve when it fits our schedule—but moved to be true servants. Galatians 2:20 explains how this type of compassion is possible. "I have been crucified with Christ and I no longer live, but Christ lives in me. The life I live in the body, I live by faith in the Son of God, who loved me and gave himself for me."

One word of caution. As the saying goes, "Be careful

---

1. Richard Foster, *Celebration of Discipline* (San Francisco: Harper, 1988), 129-30.

what you ask for; you just might get it." Being filled with Christ's compassion will cost. It will most definitely cost our time but possibly much more. It could cost our plans, our dreams, or our comfort zones. Priorities and agendas will change. We may even gain a reputation of being a little bit fanatical (as happened to Jesus and His disciples).

We can't really know where opening ourselves up to God might lead. Living compassionate lives might cause us to go to other countries as missionaries. Or it might lead us to urban areas to become community builders. Or we might go to isolated rural areas as bearers of hope and light. The price of compassion is high. Compassion has been described as "your pain in my heart."[2] When we make room for others in our lives, we take on their pain as our pain.

Opening Our Lives to Others

If we are serious, we need to be ready for our attitudes toward others to change. God's compassion will challenge our current ways of thinking. When Jesus saw the crowds, He was filled with compassion and moved to action.

When we see the crowds, we lock our car doors, grab our children, buy houses farther away. When we see the crowds, we grow indignant as to why they don't work harder, keep their yards cleaner, or, basically, just be more like us. As true servants, we will spend less time deciding who deserves help and more time simply helping. Jesus calls us to love others, even when we don't approve of their values or actions.

Since we won't be governed by results, we will not become bitter or discouraged when results fall below expectations. God requires us to serve. If we do that, then expectations have been met.

An amazing feature in our churches today is how we

---

2. Gretchen Gaebelein Hull, "Your Pain in My Heart," *Christianity Today*, February 11, 1991, 26-28.

separate Christianity from compassion. We devise a church structure and then fit Jesus' type of compassion into it as simply another program. Our church schedules often leave us little time for this type of ministry. Why are we attending the church we do? More often than not, church choice is based on what meets our personal needs rather than what serves God.

Opening Our Lives to Our Own Circle

Harder than being Jesus to those we don't know is being Jesus to our family and friends. Compassion begins at home. Nevertheless, it's much easier to help strangers than to open ourselves up to the ones to whom we are most vulnerable.

We can only fully offer God to others as we face our own, sometimes inadequate, personal relationships. Just as Jesus found no respect in His hometown, we often find it most difficult to be real to our own relationship circles. Addressing the needs of others is much easier than addressing the spiritual, physical, and emotional needs of ourselves and our families. If God's love can change the lives of others, why can't it change ours as well?

A few years ago my family was facing some very difficult situations. No one knew some of the details of these difficulties. As I was sitting in church one Sunday with my complex problems, I looked around at my church family. Although they were very loving and caring people, I knew they had no idea of our struggles.

My eyes were then opened to the fact that everyone I was looking at was probably struggling just as we were. The problems were different, but the struggles were the same. We worshiped God together yet left without ever being touched by each other's compassion.

Jesus' ministry was centered on compassion. In Matthew 25:41-43, He states plainly this compassion is required from anyone seeking entrance into the kingdom of heaven. "Then he will say to those on his left, 'Depart from me, you who are cursed, into the eternal fire prepared for the devil and his angels. For I was hungry and you gave me nothing to eat, I was thirsty and you gave me nothing to drink, I was a stranger and you did not invite me in, I needed clothes and you did not clothe me, I was sick and in prison and you did not look after me.'"

Not a single deed such as murder, adultery, or theft is mentioned here. Rather, these are sins of neglect, sins of omission. Jesus is denouncing those who do nothing.

When I respond compassionately to people, I am responding to Jesus. Then the reverse must also be true. When I ignore opportunities to display compassion, I am ignoring Jesus. Will my compassion pass the test?

A Look at Ourselves

Here are some things to consider:

1. What should this quality of Jesus' compassion do to us? How should we be responding? (We must work at our compassion in stages. Beginning in our homes, then moving into the church, and finally with strangers.)

2. The first step is accepting God's gift. Being a servant also means being able to accept service from others. Until we can be real with ourselves and God, He will never be able to work through us.

3. We then need to honestly measure our compassion. What does service look like in the routine of our daily lives? What does it look like at home, at church, in our community?

4. Think about how you respond to people:

- Do you see people or problems?
- Do you have faith or fear?
- Are you going to give time or talk?
- Are you hostile or hospitable to people different from you?

5. If we are God's representative to those in need, what kind of God do people see?

- A judging God?
- A God too busy with church activities to get involved?
- A God who only shows up on special occasions?

Remember, Jesus didn't help everyone He came in contact with during His ministry. He surely passed many by. Those He fed were hungry the next day. The people He healed eventually grew old and died. We won't be able to do everything, but that's not an excuse to do nothing.

About the author: Rev. Patty Craft is a freelance writer living in Kansas City. She is an administrative assistant at Hope Center Church of the Nazarene.

Chapter 8

Sometimes Love Hurts

by David L. Vardaman

A Look at the Characteristic
Jesus showed deep passion;
He was not afraid to show emotion.

A Look at Scripture
John 11:1-36

A Look at Jesus

A pride of lions stalks a herd of grazing zebras. As a lone zebra drifts away from the herd, the lions move closer, crouching low, then suddenly spring into action. In minutes, it's lunchtime for the lions.

Of all the nature programs I've watched on television, I don't remember ever seeing a herd hang their heads in sorrow or lift their voices in a bellowing rage when one of them is killed. Instead, they run away, leaving the unfortunate one to fend alone. They don't run for miles, just a few hundred yards, often stopping within sight of the feasting pride. They may occasionally glance toward the lions, but one has the impression that they are thinking of self-preservation, not mourning a fallen brother or sister.

Some Christians seem to think believers should greet life and death with a similar nonchalance. If someone reacts strongly to injustice, they may say, "Don't get so upset." If death claims a loved one, they may say, "Your husband is with Jesus. You should be rejoicing!" Or, "God must have needed your little girl in heaven more than you needed her here on earth."

Jesus never talked like this. Those with easy explanations for suffering and grief probably haven't suffered or grieved. Neither have they understood Jesus' deep, passionate response to life and death. Jesus never modeled the "zebra" attitude—standing stoic and aloof. Instead, He was "deeply distressed" (Mark 3:5; 14:33), He sighed deeply (Mark 7:34) and was "deeply moved" (John 11:33, 38). He also issued a stern warning (Matthew 9:30) and on another occasion a "strong warning" (Mark 1:43). Notice that in each instance, Christ's emotional response is reported at a heightened level. This is communicated in the NIV by the use of the words "deeply" and "strong" or "stern." Our Lord felt deeply and acted with emotion—and so should His disciples!

One prominent example of Jesus' deep emotional response is found in John 11:1-36. In verse 3, Mary and Martha send a message to Him saying, "Lord, the one you love is sick." Who did they mean? It seems that their message might easily have been misinterpreted, since at least three people lived in their house. Apparently Jesus enjoyed a deep friendship with Lazarus, and it was to this that they alluded. The word translated "love" here is the Greek *phileo*, often used to communicate friendship or a deep personal attachment.

Similarly, in the Gospel of John, an unnamed disciple is referred to three times as "the disciple whom Jesus loved" (13:23; 21:7, 20). Who was this disciple? The context yields no clues, but scholars believe it was John, author of the Gospel, referring to himself in the third person. If so, he, too, is claiming a special friendship with Christ that was different than the friendship Jesus had with others.

In these examples, Jesus is seen as the Christ who loved everyone enough to lay down His life for all of them but who also had a special affection for certain close friends.* Lazarus was one of those friends.

It is important to establish that Jesus loved Lazarus deeply, for this influenced His response to the message from Mary and Martha. If Lazarus was a dear friend, not just a passing acquaintance, Jesus would want to do for His friend everything He could, as soon as He could. In fact, immediate action was Christ's modus operandi (method of procedure). In John 9, He immediately healed the man born blind, the man of whom He said, "This [blindness] happened so that the work of God might be displayed in his life" (v. 3). Even when He was displaying the "work of God" in a man's life, He moved quickly. How much faster would He move when a dear friend was suffering? Still, He did not move quickly. His inaction created a tension we can feel.

If we read John 11:4-6 pensively and slowly, we do not hear Jesus confidently declaring that Lazarus will be all right. Rather, it is as if Jesus was realizing at that moment what God wanted to do, as if Jesus was just then deciding not to rush to Bethany. This pensive, hesitant interpretation seems right in the light of verse 6, which says, "Yet when he heard that Lazarus was sick, he stayed where he was two more days." This is John's surprise at Jesus' puzzling behavior. Every precedent, every social custom, and every dictate of friendship called Jesus to rapid response, to start for Bethany right away. Yet He stayed where He was, and John felt the tension too.

Then in verse 7, Jesus spoke, saying to His disciples, "Let us go back to Judea." The disciples had wondered why Jesus didn't rush back to Bethany but had satisfied themselves with a plausible explanation—returning to

---

*For further study, review the following passages that use the same word for love *(phileo)* as used in John 11:3: see John 5:20; 12:25; 1 Corinthians 16:22; Titus 3:15; and Revelation 3:19.

Bethany would put His life in jeopardy. We know this is what they thought, for when He called them to action, they protested, "But Rabbi, . . . a short while ago the Jews tried to stone you" (v. 8).

In reply, Jesus said, somewhat enigmatically, "Are there not twelve hours of daylight? A man who walks by day will not stumble, for he sees by this world's light. It is when he walks by night that he stumbles, for he has no light" (vv. 9-10).

What did Jesus mean by this? Did the disciples understand? He might have been saying:

- "Yes, there is danger in returning to Bethany, but we'll travel in the daytime and minimize the danger."
- Or, "Just as a day only has so many hours of light, so I have only a limited time in which to work. My crucifixion is not far away. While I still have opportunity, I must do God's work. To stay here in fear is to waste time and invite worse troubles."
- Or, "I am the Light of the World. My plans are not based on dark human understanding and chance but on God's will, which has been made clear to me. To walk according to God's will is like walking in the daytime. To walk according to mere human intuition is like walking in the dark."

Whatever the specific meaning, Jesus sets aside the disciples' protest, saying in verse 11, "Our friend Lazarus has fallen asleep; but I am going there to wake him up."

The disciples protested again, still thinking of safety. Jesus said plainly, "Lazarus is dead, and for your sake I am glad I was not there, so that you may believe. But let us go to him" (vv. 14-15).

Earlier, Jesus seemed to feel pulled in two directions, wanting to go to Lazarus immediately yet sensing that God willed a delay. Now, Jesus fully accepted the delay and saw how it might deepen the disciples' belief. However, the disciples don't have Jesus' understanding or His sense of anticipation. They accompanied Him to Bethany in the mood of making a funeral home visit. They had no vision of the resurrection possibilities. This was just a visit to console the grieving, and some of them thought they were going to meet death themselves.

When Jesus arrived in Bethany, Lazarus *was* dead—and had been for four days. In her grief, Martha rebuked Jesus. "If you had been here, my brother would not have died. But I know that even now God will give you whatever you ask" (vv. 21-22).

While her rebuke was softened by "even now God will give you whatever you ask," Martha certainly was saying, "Lord, You've let us down—not only Mary and me but Lazarus too!"

Mary's greeting was also a rebuke. "Lord, if you had been here, my brother would not have died" (v. 32). John recorded these rebukes as words from the hearts of hurting people to the only One who could set things right. Martha and Mary spoke out of pain, not unbelief.

Here is where the "zebra" people would insert their stiff-upper-lip counsel, but Jesus said nothing of the kind. He didn't respond to their words. He responded to their pain and asked, "Where have you laid him?" (v. 34). Instead of scolding or scowling, Jesus hurt with them. He spoke the truth, but He spoke as a fellow sufferer. There is a world of difference between declaring the truth as a prophet, preacher, or parent and speaking the truth as a fellow sufferer. The former communicates judgment and distance; the latter, compassion and partnership in suffering. This is the spirit that we find so warm and comforting in the 23rd psalm.

In verse 35 of John 6, the shortest one in the Bible, Jesus' pain registers plainly as John writes, "Jesus wept." So simple. So elegant. So human. Yet, He was the Son of God!

In the New Testament, Jesus is shown weeping only twice, here and again in Luke 19:41. He wept here because of the human condition and the havoc of death and loss. In Luke 19 He wept over Jerusalem because of the blindness and stubbornness that sin brings to the human heart. He wept because they had rejected the only One who could help them.

These scenes say that Jesus was capable of public tears. That we see Him crying only twice tells us it wasn't a daily habit, nor did He use tears to manipulate. That we see Him cry more than once emphasizes His tears as if to say, "See, godly men (and women) do cry. And sometimes, when love hurts enough, they even cry in public."

Not everyone was moved by Jesus' compassion. Some in the crowd understood His tears as a sign of His love for Lazarus, while others (the "zebras") said, in effect, "Why didn't He do something? Tears are no good. He should have come earlier and healed the man!"

This isn't the whole story, but it is enough to show our Lord's depth of emotion. Notice what He experienced to this point in the story:

- Sadness at Lazarus being sick
- Compassion for Lazarus and his sisters
- Confidence that all would be well and God glorified
- Calm in taking His time getting to Lazarus
- Frustration with the disciples who did not grasp the spiritual realities of the situation
- Disappointment that Martha and Mary had given in to despair
- Assurance that God would give Him whatever He asked
- Grief at the death of His close friend Lazarus

The ancient Stoics aimed for life without emotions. For them, the highest virtue was experiencing life's extremities without reflecting it emotionally—loss without feeling or showing grief, success without pride or joy. This wasn't Christ's way, and it isn't Christian. He gave us a richer example than the zebras. He rejoiced with the newlyweds in John 2 and wept with the grief-stricken at the tomb of Lazarus. Those who argue for a passionless Christianity deny our passionate Lord. The New Testament shows Him to be a man of many emotions, including the so-called darker emotions of indignation, sorrow, and distress. He felt all these things, and He was always without sin.

A Look at Life

Many Christians handle grief in a Christlike way; others completely stumble over it. It is important for us to accept grief for what it is—God's way of helping us cope with loss. We may grieve over the death of a loved one, the loss of a job, the loss of a limb, or anything that we once possessed and now possess no longer. If we do not deny our loss but face it, feel it, and finally accept it, this is the process of grieving.

Some Christians are good at helping others move through this process, but others need to watch Christ more closely and imitate Him. From John 11, we can observe and imitate these steps to helping another cope with loss:

- *Go to the grieving person.* Sometimes we stay away thinking, "I wouldn't know what to say." Actually, it is more important for us to *be with* our grieving friends than to say anything *to* them.

- *Do not respond defensively to emotion-laden words.* Just as Jesus let the "attacking" words of Martha and Mary pass without defending himself, we, too, ought to sidestep words spoken out of hurt and loss. Sometimes the best reply to such words is simply to say, "It hurts a lot, doesn't it?"

- *Speak words of biblical truth as a fellow sufferer, not as a prophet.* "I keep reminding myself that we will see this loved one in heaven" sounds far more comforting than, "The Bible says that this isn't the end. Buck up!"

- *Encourage the bereaved to talk.* Let them talk about the departed loved one or about news events of the day or whatever. Resist the temptation to force them to "be serious" or to "lighten up," to talk about the deceased or to avoid talking about the deceased. Our job as caregivers is to comfort, not direct the conversation. So, we might find ourselves at the side of a casket, laughing uproariously with the family as they recall a humorous incident from the life of the deceased. Yet, before the laughter dies away, we might also hear something like, "We had such fun together! Why is he gone? Why?"

- *Don't be afraid to show sorrow.* Jesus wept, and so may we.

Most Christians don't deny that emotions are as natural to life as breathing. The Christian Church, in general, is not out to make Stoics of everyone. Even in Holiness churches, we sometimes struggle with strong emotions such as anger.

We may know Ephesians 4:26 by heart ("'In your anger do not sin': Do not let the sun go down while you are still angry"), which says it is possible to be angry and not sin, but we are not always good at being angry appropriately. Cain was violently angry with Abel. Jonah was angry that a worm had killed the vine that shaded him. The disciples were angry enough to call down fire from heaven upon a Samaritan village. Cain, Jonah, and the disciples all displayed sinful, inappropriate anger. Sometimes, like them, our most heated anger is generated by similar situations. We become angry when someone is elected to a position of leadership that we wanted for ourselves, when the air conditioning fails, or when we are rejected or insulted.

Jesus was incapable of this kind of anger, for it is rooted in selfishness and ego. Cain was angry because he believed that Abel, who gave God a pleasing offering, had made his own offering look less desirable. Can you imagine Jesus ever blaming others for His own shortcomings (indeed, He was without sin or flaw)? Jonah's anger was rooted in racial prejudice. He was angry at God for sending him to Nineveh and for saving the wicked Ninevites, who deserved nothing but punishment—in Jonah's opinion. Can you imagine Jesus being angry when people believed in Him and repented of their sins? Never! The disciples' anger in Luke 9 is rooted in the pride of thinking, "You can't treat our Master like this!" They were angry because the Samaritans had rejected Jesus. They wanted to destroy them, but Jesus was merciful, graceful, and full of love. He wanted "everyone to come to repentance" (2 Peter 3:9).

What, then, angered Jesus? False religion for one thing, making it difficult for people to come to God for another, and "using" people for a third. Since Jesus could not be sinfully angry, anytime He was angry it was righteous, appropriate as an example for us to follow.

Notice also that He chose to direct His anger against foundational issues, not surface issues. He never said anything about hand washing or haircutting. Appearances really don't tell us what is going on deep inside. Anger at mere appearances is like powdering over a malignant mole. It may look better, but it is still a killer. It has to come out. Powder isn't enough. Surgery is required. For example, the elder brother of the prodigal gave every appearance of being righteous, loyal, and faithful, but his heart was full of anger and hatred. He needed some "spiritual surgery."

How can we develop a Christlike use of anger?

- *Pray for God to interrupt our "leaps to anger" so that we have time to think twice before exploding.* When God does this, we will experience the same stimulus, but we will ask, "Do I want to become angry at this? Is it worth it? Will my anger please God?" In that split second we can decide, with the help of the Spirit, not to follow our usual patterns of anger.

- *Keep a list of what causes anger and then examine the list.* Ask, "Are these foundational or frivolous issues? Will they matter a year from now, a hundred years from now? Are any of these issues of injustice, mercy, and grace? Which are connected to a sense of pride and ego?"

- *Consult with a pastor or trusted Christian friend.* Ask this person to help us think through why we become angry over what is relatively unimportant.

- *Ask God to work in our hearts through His Holy Spirit to free us from pride-centered anger and move us to redirect our anger against that which matters* (such as pornography, abortion on demand, and the increasing "heathen darkness" right here in our culture).

A Look at Ourselves

Questions about grief:

- When you have experienced grief, what one thing did another say or do that was of great comfort to you? What one thing was especially not helpful?

- In your opinion, how long is the normal grieving process: one year, one month, one lifetime? (True grief knows no time limit. It may wax and wane unexpectedly. The error is to expect that you will get to the point where you are "completely over" a significant loss.)

- How do you express deep sorrow?

- What are some appropriate ways for Christians to express grief? Why are these more appropriate than others?

- What are some inappropriate ways for Christians to express grief? Why are these less appropriate than others?

Questions about anger:

- How do you express your anger?
- What moves you to anger?
- Make a list of the things that make you angry, and then label them with an *F* for foundational or an *E* for ego. (Refer to discussion above for definitions of the two terms.)

Devotional exercises:

- In prayer, acknowledge that God made you a complete human being, including your capacity for strong emotion.
- Next, begin speaking to God about your emotions. Do you feel out of control, too angry, and so forth? Tell Him. Do you feel unable to grieve, to love, to express even righteous anger? Tell Him.
- Ask God to show you the root cause of any emotional hampering and the solution. Tell God you want to be like Jesus, capable of enjoying and using all the best that He put in you.

About the author: David Vardaman is the pastor of The Wesleyan Church in Gastonia, North Carolina. He is married and the father of two children. He enjoys reading, writing, photography, and walking. He is a graduate of Indiana Wesleyan University and Western Michigan University.

CHAPTER 9

GETTING AWAY FOR A WHILE

by James Bryan Smith

A Look at the Characteristic
Jesus used times of solitude for spiritual renewal.

A Look at Scripture
Mark 1:35

A Look at Jesus

Jesus was a busy person. He healed. He taught. He traveled. He ate. He attended weddings, interrupted funerals, exorcized demons, calmed storms, walked on water, and debated with religious leaders.

And you thought you were busy!

Yet, Jesus did one thing, one very important thing, that you and I are reluctant to do—rest. We live in a culture that makes us feel guilty if we relax. In order to be important, to feel worthy, we need to be doing something. We are pressed from all sides, and we cannot seem to get off of the endless treadmill of activity.

Jesus knew better. He understood the importance of solitude. He knew that in order to live a faithful life before God He would need as much inactivity as activity. He frequently went off by himself to quiet places, not because He was an introvert, but because He needed refreshment.

What He knew—yet so few of us really understand—is the principle of *dependence.* He lived His life entirely on the strength of the Father. "Don't you believe that I am in the Father, and that the Father is in me? The words I say to you are not just my own. Rather, it is the Father, living in me, who is doing his work" (John 14:10).

Notice that phrase, "It is the Father, living in me, who is doing his work." Jesus lived a life of dependence, completely reliant on the power of the Father who dwelled in Him. When we see Jesus going about His ministry, seemingly without becoming tired, we are prone to think, "Well, He was divine! No wonder He could heal people from dawn till dusk without a break." Thinking this way is wrong for two reasons.

First, it denies the humanity of Jesus. Jesus was fully human. He was also fully divine, but He was not superhuman because of His divine nature. His heart beat just as ours, His legs grew weary going up a steep hill, and He needed sleep as badly as any of us.

Second, it fails to take seriously what I call the transitional phrases in the Gospel stories. Transitional phrases tell us the movement of the story. *"After he had dismissed [the crowd],* he went up on a mountainside by himself to pray" (Matthew 14:23, emphasis added). *"After leaving them,* he went up on a mountainside to pray" (Mark 6:46, emphasis added). *"At daybreak* Jesus went out to a solitary place" (Luke 4:42, emphasis added).

At first glance, these transitional phrases seem unnecessary and unimportant, as if the biographer were merely finding a way to introduce the next story or parable or healing. In fact, it is quite the opposite. They are crucial. There are no wasted words in the Bible. When Matthew tells us that Jesus went up the mountain by himself or Luke lets us know that He departed to a deserted place, they are giving us valuable information about Jesus. Apparently Jesus did this kind of thing often enough that His disciples remembered it. In fact, the Gospels record 14 times of "getting away" in Jesus' three-year ministry (Matthew 14:13; 14:23; Mark 1:12-13 [also parallel passages Matthew 4:1-2 and Luke 4:1-2]; 1:35; 6:32; 14:32; Luke 4:42; 5:16; 6:12; 9:10; 9:28; 11:1; John 6:15; 11:54).

It was Jesus' way of living. He knew that in order to do the things He was called to do, He would need to withdraw from the crowds, get away from the hurry, hustle, and needs. Why? To be refreshed, energized, and reconnected to the Father's power, life, and wisdom.

While many of us simply push harder and harder when things become busy, Jesus did the opposite. Take, for example, our primary Bible passage for this session, Mark 1:35. If we look at the previous verses, we will notice that Jesus had just spent the night touching and talking with people, healing them, and caring for their needs. This, no doubt, took tremendous energy out of Jesus.

A woman once touched the hem of His garment in order to be healed, and even that, Jesus noted, took power from Him. He felt the energy go out from Him. This happened each time He was involved in healing. "The people all tried to touch him, because *power was coming from him* and healing them all" (Luke 6:19, emphasis added).

So in our key passage, Jesus had just spent many hours healing people. You can just imagine how the people were pressing in on Him. Wouldn't you, if you or a loved one were sick and you heard stories of a man who was healing people? I think all of us would flock to this person and stay at his doorstep until he would take care of us. This is why it went on late into the night.

But what next? Most of us would collapse and try to find a place to sleep. Notice what Jesus did. Let's look at Mark 1:35 again more carefully. "Very early in the morning, while it was still dark, Jesus got up, left the house and went off to a solitary place, where he prayed."

After a long night, before the sun came up, Jesus got up and went to a deserted place. The Greek word Mark used to describe this place is translated "lonely" (RSV), "deserted" (PHILLIPS), or "solitary" (KJV, NIV). No matter which you prefer, the important point is that it was a quiet place. No one else was around.

That is the key point here—Jesus needed to be alone. When we are with other people, we must give them our attention. That is what it means to be in the presence of others—to be attentive to them, to their words, to their needs. However, now it was time for something else, or rather Someone else, to grasp His attention.

Mark tells us that He went to this lonely, quiet, deserted place, not merely to take a nap but to pray. For many of us, prayer is a little like lifting a list of requests to God, a wish list containing the things we need, or simply want, God to do for us. This is not the kind of prayer that Jesus was engaged in—at least not entirely.

I am sure that He spoke to the Father directly about all kinds of needs, different problems He was facing, and perplexing struggles He was engaged in. More than that, I imagine that the majority of this time was spent in silent adoration and quiet contemplation. In the midst of the stillness comes a gentle Voice that whispers, "I am with You. You are My beloved Son. Trust in My strength."

The startling thing about Jesus' way of praying was the intimacy with which He prayed. If we read the great prayer of the 17th chapter of John's Gospel, we will see a person addressing God with great familiarity and trust. He spoke to the Father with candor and honesty; He lifted His prayer with certainty that God heard Him and would answer His request.

This is why it is so important for us to look at Jesus as our Example. He was busy and certainly felt drained physically. Instead of tumbling into bed, He escaped the crowd for a time of solitude. He knew how to get refreshed and realigned with the life and power that flowed through Him. Here is what is so ironic: most of us, when busy, neglect solitude and prayer. Yet for Jesus, it was just the opposite. When He was pressed and stressed, He retreated to be alone with God for prayer.

After a time of solitude, He was again ready to go back and resume the active work of ministry. His disciples, who no doubt had gone to sleep, awoke to find Jesus missing. Their first reaction was to panic and scurry about trying to find Him. When they did find Him, Jesus casually replied that it was time to head to another town to proclaim the Good News.

We see in Jesus that beautiful rhythm of action and contemplation, of work and rest, of noise and silence, of being with people and getting away for a time of solitude. Jesus was the wisest person who ever lived, and He knew how life should be lived. When we examine those "transitional phrases"—such as "he withdrew" or "he went up on a mountainside by himself"—we are given a glimpse into how Jesus lived and, consequently, how we ought to live as well.

It was not just for himself. Jesus instructed His disciples to do the same and would often take them with Him for times of rest and refreshment. They, too, were involved in the taxing work of caring for the poor and the sick and proclaiming the message of the Kingdom to many who did not want to hear. They, too, needed rest. Jesus not only modeled it for them but also involved them in it.

For example, He took a few of His closest disciples with Him during a very important moment in His ministry. "About eight days after Jesus said this, he took Peter, John and James with him and went up onto a mountain to pray" (Luke 9:28). Jesus took them away from the rest of the people in order to let them engage in a time of silence and prayer. It also became a time for deeper discussion and a time to care for them more specifically.

This, too, is a great example to all of us. We need times of solitude, not merely for us as individuals but also for us as a community. Small gatherings of people who retreat, as

Jesus and these three disciples did, are able to truly become present to one another and really listen to each other. Jesus, ever the compassionate and caring Leader, knew that to lead people into the deeper life He would not only need to model it but also need to invite people into it.

A Look at Life

We live in a busy world. In fact, it is getting harder and harder for people to rest and relax in today's fast-paced, jam-packed society. Ironically, in the 1960s, futurists were examining the rise of technology and theorizing about its effects on people's lives. They heard about such things as microwave ovens, fax machines, and computer networking. They concluded that by the end of the 1990s people would have more leisure time than ever because all of these "timesaving" devices would leave us free to do other things. They predicted four-day workweeks and eight-week vacations.

How wrong they were. People have less leisure time than ever before. We are working longer days and taking fewer vacations. The timesaving devices have not saved time, they have only increased the speed at which we do things. In fact, because of the increased capabilities that technology has created, we have to work harder in order to stay up with our competitors and struggle to keep up with the new technology lest ours becomes obsolete.

This has had a dramatic effect on our souls. We are tired. We have pushed ourselves beyond our limits, and as a result, many people are failing to enjoy life. What is even worse is the fact that we have lost the ability to hear God. We are too busy, and there is too much noise. The still, small voice of God gets drowned out by our many pursuits, by stereos around our heads, by 75 television channels, and by 50-hour workweeks.

Even our church services have become filled with noise. We are busy moving from hymn to prayer, to praise singing, to another prayer and a sermon, and then to a benediction. There is no stillness. There is no silence. Sometimes God cannot be heard, and we correspondingly cannot become our true selves.

When we are so frantic and our lives are so filled, we are forced to become false persons. We cannot live out of our true selves but instead create personae (images) that others, we assume, will like and accept. For example, we all know that we behave differently around different people. None of those "persons" is our true self, though some come closer than others. Only solitude can help us take off the masks. This is why solitude is so important, because it breaks us out of the patterns and representations that have held us captive.

Solitude is simply this: choosing to step away from human relationships for a period of time—usually for a few hours—in order to make room for God. These relationships, while good, healthy, and normal, can also be inhibiting. Stepping away from them, for a time, allows us to focus on God. We are not pretending, we are not acting, we are simply *being*.

The payoff of solitude is how we are when we reenter. We are usually relaxed, more in sync, and less flustered by trivial matters. We are better listeners, more attentive to people, and we have a greater awareness of the power of God that surrounds us and sustains all that we do. This means that we walk with more confidence and are willing to lean more and more on God's available resources.

The fruit of solitude is that we are able to be with God wherever we are. A person who has experienced real solitude will never be lonely again. It is also a cure for busyness. We begin to see the almost comical ways we hurry through much of life and miss so much of what is going on around us.

My friend told me about a dog on the farm where he grew up. The dog had a terrible problem. He liked to bite the front tire of a tractor—when it was moving! Consequently, the dog would get run over by the back tire. He would then go into the house, lay down, and heal for four days. Then he would get up, go back, and do it again!

We are a lot like that. We go out, get busy, wear ourselves out, and then have to collapse somewhere (or get sick, which is a way of forcing us to rest). God never intended us to live this way. We were designed to live in the rhythmic pattern of action and contemplation. We were created to engage in activities and be with people but then to get away, rest, and learn to be attentive to God in the stillness.

A few years ago I made a commitment to spend time in solitude. An old friend of mine and her husband decided to turn a room near their farmhouse into a *poustinia*, a Russian word that describes a place for quiet and rest, even in the midst of the city. Making this room available to people is a ministry to which they have been called.

A couple of times a month I go out to their farm and spend four or five hours there alone. I sit, look out the window, and watch the wheat blow in the wind. I sip a cup of tea or take a short nap. I read the Bible, I pray, and I write in my journal. Mostly I do nothing. I simply rest in God.

These are some of the richest times I have ever had on this earth. Though it takes time, within a few hours I enter into a feeling of quiet peace, and I take down the barriers between myself and God (usually through times of relaxed yet honest and searching confession). I stop hurrying. I start listening.

I imagine that this is something similar to what Jesus did. When I reenter my normal life (of diapers, dishrags, and deadlines), I do so with new eyes and new ears. My children look more wonderful, my wife more beautiful, and my life more precious than it did before. They say the proof of the pudding is in the eating. I say that the real value of getting away for solitude is found in what it will do for your life. Taste and see that the Lord is good.

A Look at Ourselves

Questions:

1. Why did Jesus feel it necessary to withdraw from the crowds and be alone?

2. What are some of the reasons why people are so busy? Why do we push ourselves so hard?

3. What are some of your reservations about spending time alone? Does it sound frightening and impossible? Why?

4. What is one benefit of "getting away" that you would most like to have in your life (i.e., peace, clearer connection with God, deeper appreciation of yourself and your world)?

5. How could you begin to practice solitude, even in your life situation?

Exercises:

1. Set aside 10 minutes each morning for a time of silence. Grab a warm cup of something good and just look out the window.

2. Schedule a lengthy period (three hours or more) to go to a quiet place by yourself. A library, a chapel, or a place out in nature (weather permitting) can become a sanctuary of quiet for you. Use this time to talk and listen to God. Allow your life perspective to be shaped and refreshed by this human-divine interaction.

3. Take a prayer walk with someone. Try not to say anything to your partner for much of the journey, but at some point turn to one another and share what is on your heart. Labor to listen attentively, and conclude your time together with prayer.

About the author: Dr. James Bryan Smith is chaplain and assistant professor of philosophy at Friends University in Wichita, Kansas.

Chapter 10

Forgiving for Living

by Mark A. Holmes

A Look at the Characteristic
Jesus was a forgiving person and taught His followers to forgive.

A Look at Scripture
Matthew 18:15-35

A Look at Jesus
It had been a long and well-publicized trial. The lawyers had finished presenting their cases, and the matter was turned over to the jurors. I was watching the proceedings on television. Filling the airtime while the jury was out, a reporter asked what the victim's family was doing while they waited. A friend responded, "They are a deeply religious family. They are home praying that he will get what he deserves."

The response struck me with its contradiction. My human nature understood well what these people were seeking, yet my Christian nature was shouting, "Something is wrong here!" This is not what Jesus would have sought. His words "Father, forgive them, for they do not know what they are doing" (Luke 23:34) and "Neither do I condemn you. . . . Go now and leave your life of sin" (John 8:11) came to mind.

Jesus came to earth for a number of reasons, but the main purpose was to procure salvation for all who believe, salvation that would result from God forgiving us of our sins. Jesus' ministry would need to provide not only the means of forgiveness but also the pattern by which His followers would be able to both receive and express this gift.

How is this possible? How do we move beyond the desire for judgment and condemnation to a more Christlike expression of forgiveness and grace? What was there about Jesus and His nature that enabled Him to forgive people as He did? How do we establish these attributes within our own lives? The 18th chapter of Matthew is very helpful in answering these questions. It is an extended discussion by Jesus regarding the exercise of grace toward one another. He reveals three major understandings that must be held by people who hope to live like Him: (1) In relating people to people, we must recognize *equality*. (2) In relating people to the law, we must recognize *priority*. (3) In relating people to God, we must recognize *liability*.

The Equality of People

The topic of equality is introduced earlier in chapter 18 of Matthew through a question posed by the disciples regarding who is the greatest in the kingdom of heaven. Though the connection between greatness and forgiveness may not be immediately obvious, the relationship is unmistakable. Judgment is only possible when one establishes levels of superiority. The supremacy of one allows for the judgment of another. The wider the distinction, the easier judgment may be expressed. Jesus dispels this superiority issue by illustration and parable.

He illustrates equality by placing a child before the inquiring disciples as an example of greatness. In doing so, He turned the hierarchy of His day upside down, making what society viewed as the least, the greatest. Jesus' teaching expressed that superiority in the Kingdom was determined by different criteria than in the world. Superiority could not be determined by age or position but by childlike humility. In the world, pride and superiority may walk hand in hand, but in the kingdom of God, superiority's companion is humility.

Jesus continued to press His teaching home on this topic by sharing a parable illustrating that superiority could not be determined by number. What is more important, the masses or the individual? Even today we stress the superiority of size. We feel it reflects greatness, success, authority. However, by telling the parable of the lost sheep, Jesus taught that one lost individual took precedence over 99 others that were saved. This move from the masses to the individual continues to challenge us today. It has been said that we view our church services as 1 congregation of 100, but Jesus views it as 100 congregations of 1. Jesus is not impressed by our size but by our concern for the individual. This point is made clear in our scripture passage as Jesus places great stress on the care and concern of the individual person. He speaks of a brother who sins—not a group, a town, or a society. The sins of one individual become a major concern for the follower of Christ.

Jesus gives some rather specific and pointed instructions regarding the way we are to handle those among us who commit acts of sin. His message reveals that the one who is *not* guilty of a particular infraction is of no greater significance than the one who is. In fact, the sinner is to be restored by the innocent, even if the innocent was the victim of the wrong. Jesus' lifestyle and teachings revealed that superiority cannot be defined by such words as "victim" and "perpetrator," "guilty" and "innocent." People are people; some are forgiven, and others are in need of forgiveness.

This equality does not imply that we are without ability to discern between right and wrong or make a judgment regarding correct behavior. Often this error is expressed by some in saying it is not their place to judge. Or others, seeking to justify an action, say that no one has the right to judge them. We do have the right to determine the appropriateness of an action and should exercise it. However, this responsibility does not give us a means to distinguish people as much as it presents the requirement to restore the errant. Once it is determined that a person is wrong, the response is not separation but reclamation. True, at the end of Jesus' instructions, He tells us to treat the unrepentant individual as a "pagan or a tax collector" (Matthew 18:17). Nevertheless, the context implies the judgment is based on the refusal to repent, not the initial sin itself.

A closely associated issue is raised when we make a listing of sins by their severity or their number. Both of these become human means of distinction. This was apparently Peter's concern when he asked Jesus his question in verse 21. "How many times do I let them get away with it before I label them as no longer worthy of my forgiveness?" (author's paraphrase). In Peter's thinking (as well as our own), there is a limit defined by numbers but not so with Christ. The number of sins, just like the quality of sin, does not make one person less equal to us. We may be repulsed by the act committed, or even the frequency, but the person is still our equal. Only the rejection of grace and restoration, in time, can reduce the person's status.

If we are to live a life of forgiveness that exemplifies our Lord's, it must begin by our willingness to refuse the labeling of people with superior or inferior positions in life. We all carry an inherent value, an intrinsic worth, which makes us equal to one another in the eyes of God. This value was given to us by God when He created us in His image and when He purchased us by the death of His Son. Paul reminded his readers that we were "bought at a price" (1 Corinthians 6:20; 7:23). The value of an item is determined by the price one is willing to pay for it. The death of Jesus Christ has assessed our value in God's eyes. If we are to forgive as Jesus forgives, it can only begin by seeing the equal value of each individual, a value that He gave to us by dying in our place.

The Priority of People

One of the great obstacles we encounter in the area of forgiveness is created by our confusion of priorities. Which is of greater importance, the law or the person? This apparently was a stumbling block for the religious leaders of Jesus' day as was illustrated on several occasions when Jesus desired to heal people on the Sabbath. Three occasions are listed in Scripture: a woman stooped over for years with a crippled back (see Luke 13:10-16), a man with a hand withered beyond use (see Matthew 12:10), and a man with dropsy (see Luke 14:1-6). When Jesus wanted to express compassion by healing these people, He was rebuked by the leaders for breaking the Sabbath laws. In their view, the laws and their protection took precedence over people. Jesus, in indignation, pointed out their error by revealing they treated their livestock with more compassion than they did humans. Livestock could be fed, watered, and rescued from peril, but people were to be left to their suffering.

Justice deals with the protection of the person as well as the law. To harm either by our actions produces its cry against us. Justice claims, if we break the law, we must pay. Infractions cannot be overlooked without the risk of making the law impotent. Laws not upheld stand the risk of becoming ignored. This reality was well-known among the religious leaders of Jesus' day, and they placed a strong emphasis on the prevention of any law being misused or overlooked. People may have needs, but the law was the law.

Jesus had a differing view, not that the law was unimportant, but that restoration of people took a higher priority. This view of prioritizing humans above justice is apparent in His instructions to the disciples concerning the restoration of the person who sinned.

His instructions for restoration call for a multistepped approach. The first attempt is personal, because it involves one individual approaching another—whether as a victim to perpetrator or a concerned individual to another in need. The purpose for this meeting is not revenge or even justice but restoration. Reveal the fault, and if the person is open to change, "you have won your brother over" (Luke 18:15).

However, not everyone is willing to deal with his or her errors in life and may respond coldly. Our efforts are not to end there. The next appeal reflects a social attempt as one is to take along one or two additional people in an attempt to resolve the matter (v. 16). This is not a call to gang up on the guilty, but in keeping with the dictates of the law, it serves to testify of the guilt while keeping the door open for restoration. Jesus reminded them of this responsibility from Deuteronomy 19:15, which prevented any one person from being accused by another without additional witnesses. This approach reflects the beginnings of a judicial process, which grows stronger with each refusal by the guilty.

However, as redemptive as our efforts might be, some people refuse to listen to both individuals and society in regard to their wrongs, remaining in opposition. If this be the case, Jesus instructs us to take them to the next level—the church (v. 17). Again the opportunity should be allowed for the person to repent and be restored. However, if he or she refuses to heed the church in its expression of grace, the person is to be dealt with as one who rejects the grace. They are "pagan" or as despicable as a "tax collector" was in Jesus' day.

The Liability of People

One final view is necessary to enable us to forgive as Jesus did—the recognition that as humans we are all liable for sin. "For all have sinned and fall short of the glory of God" (Romans 3:23). This common liability brings the awareness that any view or attitude we might hold or express toward others on account of their sins is in effect an indictment against ourselves, since we are in the same situation. This is Jesus' message of the unmerciful steward in Matthew 18:21-35. The servant failed to make a connection between the massive debt he owed the king and the insignificant debt owed to him by another. With the king he pleads mercy, with his fellow human he exacts justice. The king's question in verse 33 is the foundational understanding for our actions: "Shouldn't you have had mercy on your fellow servant just as I had on you?"

This was the missing ingredient I recognized with the news interview mentioned at the beginning of this chapter. Here were "deeply religious people" obviously forgetting their massive debt forgiven by God while praying for vengeance upon another. Apparently, grace is the desired reaction we hope the world will take on our behalf—unless we are the victim. Then it becomes personal, and we lose a sense of our own liability. Jesus does not allow us this option. In fact, He warns us that our forgetfulness in relation to our liability could well cost us the grace we have originally received (v. 35).

Our sense of liability becomes distorted by our subjectivity. We find it impossible to forgive someone for a single incident, while we want God to forgive all our waywardness in life. Only as we keep an accurate perspective of our liability can we forgive the offenses of people against us.

In an age of grace, Jesus has revealed that people are to be dealt with equally, with an emphasis on forgiveness rather than punishment. However, this is not the final expression. There is the potential that we can thwart God's grace by outward refusal or callous disregard of the realities of grace in a person's life. Failing to recognize our common liability before God subjects us to the same abandonment as the hardened sinner who rejects God's gracious rescue. Forgiveness for the Christian is not just a passive experience where we receive God's mercy. It also must be an active work on the part of the believer, extended to others as equal in value, superior to judgment and in recognition of the common liability we all hold before our Heavenly Father.

A Look at Life

Having looked at Jesus' example and teachings, we come to the timely question, Why is His call to forgiveness so important to our present experience? The answer has three facets. First, there is a *personal* dimension. As Jesus has stated in the parable of the unmerciful servant, the need for a person to forgive others is not a suggestion but a command. Our failure to forgive people will result in the sacrifice of our own salvation. We must be willing to extend mercy if we hope to receive it.

Second, there is a *corporate* dimension. The actions of the followers of Christ must exhibit to the world the nature of Christ. Do we not contradict our message when we refuse to forgive people? Don't we distort the image of the Church when we proclaim a message of grace while living a life of judgment? There is always an attraction to pharisaism, where we exalt ourselves above others, emphasize the law, and forget the works of grace in our own lives. Such attitudes develop over time and seem natural to the human experience. However, such actions become contradictions to the gospel's claims and mar the message and mission of the Church.

Third, there is a *holiness* reason. If we understand holiness to be that transformation of the inner nature of humanity to where we love God with our whole heart and our neighbors as ourselves, then Jesus' mandate for forgiveness is a primary requirement. How can we profess a holiness experience while we express an unforgiving nature? As forgiveness is the first necessity for us to begin our relationship with God, it must also be the completing act that allows His salvation to be made complete within us. We only fool ourselves when we believe that by replacing grace and forgiveness with judgment and denouncement, we somehow reflect a holy nature. Holiness without forgiveness is legalism. Holiness expressing forgiveness is the very breath of God blowing upon an all-too-desperate world.

In 1981, an assassination attempt was made upon Pope John Paul II. The would-be assassin was arrested, tried, and convicted much as we expected. However, the media recorded the visit to the jail cell where the pope came to forgive the man who shot him. This distinction must always be the message of the Church. Let governments judge and destroy, but the Church should be recognized by its acts of restoration and mercy. If our actions do not portray our message, our hypocrisy will be our epitaph.

Recognizing the necessity of forgiveness does not make its expression easy. There are certain obstacles that we need to overcome. One major challenge is the task of overcoming our feelings of being victims. There is nothing like being hurt to make us cry out for "justice." In our litigious society, the potential for vengeance is great. If we feel victimized, our answer is to bring suit against the guilty. We can claim any number of negative experiences to validate our claim. We take away one another's wealth as a compensation for hurt, but does any financial settlement really take away the hurt? How do we move beyond being victims to being victors? By recognizing that the person who has wronged us is a valuable person. When we are hurt, it is easy to degrade our attackers, which helps us respond destructively. If we refuse to reduce their standing in our eyes, our temptation to denounce them may lessen. Second, if our concern is for their restoration in place of our vindication, our energies may take a different direction. Finally, if we remember that we were not without guilt and were worthy of being punished, we may be able to relate a more graceful expression. Such realizations may appeal to our logic but not necessarily to our heart. The mind may relay these truths, but our human nature may dictate an entirely different desire. This becomes the arena for God through His Holy Spirit to enable us to do what we ourselves cannot do.

One of the more memorable parts of Corrie ten Boom's book *The Hiding Place,* which describes her horrid experiences as a prisoner in the German concentration camps during World War II, comes near its end where she was free from the concentration camp and was busy sharing her testimony in postwar Europe. At the conclusion of one of her messages in Munich, she was approached by a man whom she immediately recognized as one of the S.S. guards who so brutally mistreated her and the others at the prison camp. Not recognizing her, the man came over to her and extended his hand while expressing his gratitude for her message. Corrie wrote that she knew, as a Christian, she should take the man's hand, but she could not find it in herself to lift her own in response. Finally, confessing to God her own inability to forgive the man, she asked God to enable her by His power. Immediately, she was able to raise her hand and shake that of her former tormentor. She said of this encounter, "When He tells us to love our enemies, He gives, along with the command, the love, itself."*

A Look at Ourselves

Here are some questions to prayerfully consider:

1. Who do you know in your life that needs to hear your forgiveness?

2. Who do you know who has strayed and needs restoration?

3. How do you view people—by a self-determined hierarchy or by Christ's evaluation expressed with His blood?

4. Are people more important to you than rules?

5. Are you aware of your indebtedness to God and His grace?

About the author: Rev. Mark A. Holmes is senior pastor of Hillview Wesleyan Church in Lock Haven, Pennsylvania.

---

*Corrie ten Boom and John and Elizabeth Sherrill, *The Hiding Place* (Old Tappan, N.J.: Fleming H. Revell Company, 1971), 238.

CHAPTER 11

DOING THE RIGHT THING

by Carl M. Leth

A Look at the Characteristic
Jesus was a righteous and holy person.

A Look at Scripture
Matthew 21:10-17

A Look at Jesus

Doing the right thing. It sounds so simple. Yet, doing the right thing is not as simple as it might seem. Not only is it often difficult to do, but it is often difficult to know what the right thing is. This is especially true when life gets pressurized by competing demands, personal stress, and opposing claims for our loyalty. Strident voices clamor for our attention and favor. Some call out enticing promises, while others threaten dark consequences. It sometimes becomes difficult to determine what the right thing is. Clarity is hard to achieve. How helpful it would be if Jesus could help us learn how to make good decisions in the intense pressure of living and keep the issues of our lives in the right perspective.

In fact, as Jesus made His way through the crowded streets of Jerusalem after His triumphal entry, He found himself in a stress-filled situation. Talk about pressure! He had just been received by the people of Jerusalem like a victorious king. Voices called out royal praise to honor Him. Yet, beyond the adulation of the crowd, Jesus heard other voices filled with rage and fear. Jesus knew that the time of His death was rapidly approaching. He was on a roller-coaster ride between adoration and condemnation, worship and betrayal.

Time was now rapidly compressing for Jesus. There would be no more quiet retreats. The pressurized course of events would allow little time for reflection and critical thinking. The gap between event and reaction was narrowing to a fine point. Jesus would be pressed to reveal himself with the raw honesty of spontaneous reactions. That may be as challenging a test as could be devised.

Into this testing field Jesus strode with boldness and purpose as He walked to the Temple. On Passover week the Temple courts were crowded with people and activity. Farmers and shepherds mixed with urban Jews in a contrast of life experiences and cultures. Looks of awe and amazement could be seen on the faces of the young and the old who had made their way to the famous Temple after a long pilgrimage. For some it would be a once-in-a-lifetime experience. Distance and poverty would prevent their ever coming again. This Temple visit would be a dream come true, the closest they could ever hope to come to the very presence of God.

The looks and sounds of awe from the pilgrims were a sharp contrast to the knowing looks of the Temple merchants. Their presence was, theoretically, a service to these unsophisticated country folk. The Temple offerings required unblemished sacrifices. If the animals pilgrims had brought or purchased along the way were not acceptable, they could not sacrifice. How convenient to have a concession available to assure the pilgrims of acceptable sacrifices. And should the pilgrims' currency be foreign, there were money changers readily available to assist them.

In practice, however, these concessions were granted by the high priests to relatives or high bidders. They were profiteers who controlled access to the Temple and, therefore, to God. Animals not purchased from them were routinely discovered to be blemished and unacceptable for sacrifice. Animals purchased at the Temple were oppressively expensive, and the currency exchange rates were excessive. The pilgrims' looks of awe were often transformed into expressions of amazement and despair. It was into this raucous scene of human distress and conflict that Jesus made His entrance, bringing His own high-stress life situation.

The scene must have been shocking. In the courtyard of the sacred Temple an outraged man began to overturn tables and drive merchants away. Coins scattering, people crying out, men shouting angrily, and animals bleating and squeaking combined to create a picture of chaos. In a voice filled with passion, Jesus denounced the money changers and merchants. They had compromised and distorted God's intended purposes for the Temple. In the place of merchants selling unblemished offerings, Jesus welcomed the blind and the lame, healing them. Access to God and His grace was opened to the blemished and broken.

What a powerful scene of righteous passion unleashed! We should be careful, however, not to interpret this scene as an emotional outburst. Certainly we can easily relate to losing our tempers—"blowing up." A superficial explanation of this event could serve to justify our emotional outbursts when they are prompted by a good cause. If that is what is happening here, then Jesus modeled action driven by emotional overload. Is that the message we are intended to learn? Is doing the right thing a product of passion overwhelming normal restraint? Or does this event in Jesus' life merit more careful attention?

Let me suggest another interpretation of this extraordinary confrontation in the Temple: Jesus was *not* moved to reaction by the emotional overload of righteous indignation. He was moved to act out of His deep sense of who He was and what His life was about. He was driven less by passion and more by purpose than we might have thought.

Christ was, in fact, making an important statement about the purpose of the Temple and God's agenda for action. His biblical citations indicate a clear understanding of what was at stake. Christ's allusion to God's house being a "house of prayer" is a reference to Isaiah 56:7. In that chapter Isaiah proclaimed God's vision for His Temple as a place of prayer for *all* people, specifically including the "eunuch" and the "foreigner." These outsiders were excluded from the Temple (and, by extension, God's redemption) because of their heritage or physical disfigurement. God, through Isaiah, declared His plan and desire to throw open the door to every person—including these outcasts. God's plan for His "house of prayer" was to make redemption and grace accessible to everyone without prohibitive barriers. Jesus' judgment was that the merchants and rulers of the Temple had perverted this divine purpose and denied God's welcoming invitation.

This condemning judgment is made clear in Christ's contrasting biblical image. Instead of a "house of prayer" that welcomes every person, the merchants and Temple leaders had created a "den of robbers." This image is drawn from Jeremiah 7:11, where the nation was condemned. The issue at stake was not primarily about theft but about using God in a self-serving way. The people were living in immorality and disobedience to God while still claiming God's protection. They were using God as a refuge of safety that enabled their immorality, much as a band of robbers would use a hiding place as a den of safe retreat. It was this misuse of the Temple and God's blessings that Jeremiah renounced. Jesus cited this accusation and applied it to the merchants and rulers of the Temple. They had perverted the use and blessing of the Temple to serve their personal ends of enrichments, status, and security.

Jesus used this dramatic confrontation to identify himself with the purposes of God (as expressed in Isaiah) to extend God's redemption to all people, including the outcast and foreigner. Jesus' work was to make God's grace accessible and available. Jesus and His ministry stand in striking contrast to the practices of the Temple and the religious leaders who had made redemption their private (and self-serving) franchise. This contrast is further confirmed by Jesus' reception and healing of the blind and the lame at the Temple. He was making the Temple a place of prayer for all nations.

A Look at Life

Among the lessons we might draw from this dramatic event is a lesson about doing the right thing. Jesus' actions —even in that pressure-filled encounter—were shaped by His deep sense of who He was and what His life was about. His response to that Temple scene was determined long beforehand in the formation of His personal purpose and priorities. He was able to do the right thing because His heart was right.

We live in a culture of methodologies. We worship how-tos. We would like to find a plan for knowing and doing the right thing. Jesus models a different approach altogether. His life teaches us that it's not the *plan*, it's the *Man*. The key to discerning the right thing and doing it begins with a heart that is in tune with God and a character that is clearly centered on God's values. Jesus shows us that even the most stress-filled and chaotic situation can be successfully managed when we know who we are and what we are about.

Charles Colson tells the story of a man who helped to spark the downfall of Communism in Romania. His name is Laszlo Tokes, and he was pastor of an evangelical church in Timisoara, Romania. He didn't start out to bring a government down. He simply pastored his church as faithfully as he knew how. Despite the disapproval of his superiors in the church and harassment from officials of the state, his church grew and his influence spread. Faced with threats of dismissal and arrest, he simply continued to be faithful to his calling. His obedient faithfulness prompted a spontaneous response from the people of the city and then the nation. Crowds gathered to prevent his arrest and to demonstrate their support. Finally, the police responded with violence. Tokes was beaten and arrested, and many other persons were shot. Nevertheless, the tide of events could not be turned. Within days the nation was free. Pastor Tokes never developed a strategic plan for social change. He didn't analyze the pros and cons of his options for action. What he did flowed naturally out of who he was.*

When we start from a Christ-focused center and bring a character shaped by God's values into the confusion of our life situations, we have what we need to help us know and do the right thing. We need to begin where Jesus began—investing our personal attention and effort to bring our hearts into harmony with the heart of the Father. We need to cultivate the man or woman rather than strategize a plan. It is the kind of maturity and depth of character that Paul prayed for on behalf of the Colossians, "asking God to fill [them] with the knowledge of his will through all spiritual wisdom and understanding" (1:9). When our minds, hearts, and characters are shaped by our living relationship with Christ, we are no longer being conformed to the pattern of this world but transformed according to Kingdom values. When that happens, Paul said, "you will be able to test and approve what God's will is—his good, pleasing and perfect will" (Romans 12:2).

---

*Charles Colson, *The Body: Being Light in Darkness* (Dallas: Word, 1992), 51-61.

The secret to the right choice in the midst of the pressure of life situations is our cultivation of God's presence and our being shaped by His values well before the moment of decision. When who we are is firmly focused on God's will and His plan for us, every issue we face is considered from that starting point. When the values of our lives are clearly in place, every decision we make begins with those values. When we come into the most pressurized and difficult situations of life with a strong sense of our identity and a clear commitment to purpose in Christ, we can know and do the right thing. Jesus showed us how.

A Look at Ourselves

Here are some questions to prayerfully consider:

1. Am I cultivating Christlike character by investing time with God and His Word? Is personal holiness (right relation with God) shaping who I am?

2. What would I reveal in "the raw honesty of spontaneous reactions"? What would shape my response—peer pressure, my feelings, an analysis of the situation?

3. Think about writing a personal mission and values statement. Spend some time prayerfully reflecting on your values, priorities, and personal purpose in life.

4. What "right things" do you need to do this week?

About the author: Dr. Carl Leth is senior pastor of Detroit First Church of the Nazarene.

CHAPTER 12

LIKE FATHER, LIKE SON

by David W. Holdren

A Look at the Characteristic
Jesus' life reflected God the Father.

A Look at Scripture
John 5:16-24, 30

A Look at Jesus

Ever heard the words "You remind me more and more of your father"? I receive that kind of comment occasionally. Are they referring to my nose? Or is it the changing hairline? Or is my age really starting to show? Are they referring to character, personality, or a certain behavioral trait? It leaves me with mixed feelings.

The other day I was talking with a couple about their marriage struggles. At one point the lady looked straight at her husband and blurted, "You're just like your father!" It was *not* a compliment.

Of course, not all such comparisons are negative. My chest swells when someone tells one of my daughters that they see some of *me* in them. You can imagine what my poor girls are thinking!

Here's another one: "[Jesus] is the radiance of God's glory and the exact representation of his being" (Hebrews 1:3). This is what the Bible says about Jesus' likeness to God the Heavenly Father. That is quite a statement—"like Father, like Son."

Let's get right to the point of this chapter. The Bible makes some pretty radical statements about Jesus. Actually, Jesus makes some very radical statements about himself. One such statement is found in the Bible passage cited at the beginning of this chapter. He drove some of the religious leaders of His day wild with His actions and statements.

First, Jesus was a "Sabbath-breaker." What does that mean? In those days, the Jewish scholars and religious leaders took the fourth commandment, "Remember the Sabbath day by keeping it holy" (Exodus 20:8), and got carried away with dozens of rules defining what constitutes not working on the day of rest.

Some Jews of that day were radical about the no-work thing. Some of them even refused to defend themselves if their enemies attacked on the Sabbath. They preferred being murdered to "working" on the Sabbath. Now there's a belief system to die for! Along came Jesus, healing people on the Sabbath. To some Jewish leaders that was work; therefore it was sin.

In the face of mounting accusations that Jesus was breaking the commandment, He announced one day that the Sabbath is made for humans, not humans for the Sabbath. He said it was absolutely right to do good things on that day. His contemporaries believed He deserved execution, because He was not only violating the holy day but, in the process, implying that He was equal with God.

Indeed, Jesus made some very radical statements—really "on the edge." One brilliant convert to Christ, whose name was C. S. Lewis, declared that in light of such affirmations about Christ and His divinity, a person had three choices about Jesus. He was either a liar, a lunatic, or the Lord. That about sums it up. When we choose to have personal faith in and to follow Christ, we are making a very radical decision about the one who claimed to be the Savior of the world.

When I think about this, I kind of get this impish grin inside my mind. My faith causes me to feel a bit radical and on the edge, as if I am blasting through a bunch of S curves on a motorcycle, or careening down a ski slope at breakneck speed, or doing whatever you think about doing that puts you on the edge of faith or craziness. In a very real sense, being a Christian is risking (trusting) that Jesus Christ is your best hope to make it to heaven. Wow!

Probably the most amazing claims Jesus made were about His being the very Son of God—being divine. Yet, with all of those claims about His identity, Jesus still described His relationship with God as that of Father and Son. Just as we Christians are inclined to put Jesus at the center of our lives, we must remember that Jesus put God at the center of His own life.

Jesus said that He was dependent on God the Father (see John 5:19 and 5:30). Other places in the Bible indicate that Jesus came to earth to do His Father's will or desires. The Bible affirms that the earthly life, teachings, miracles, death, and resurrection of Jesus were all dependent on the power of God the Father.

What, then, does the Bible teach about the importance of Jesus Christ? *The Message* (TM) renders John 1:14 like this: "The Word [Jesus] became flesh and blood, and moved into the neighborhood. We saw the glory with our own eyes, the one-of-a-kind glory, like Father, like Son, Generous [and gracious] inside and out, true from start to finish."

Jesus gives us a "face" for God. What is the closest we come to seeing God? Look at Jesus. By that we don't mean Jesus' physical appearance. Rather we mean His character, His teachings, His attitudes, and the way He reacted to people. That's why when we ask, "What would Jesus do?" it is like affirming that's what God would say or think or do.

The life of Jesus can teach us marvelous things that
will help develop some of our most important relationships.

A Look at Life

Not long ago I saw some news footage of Governor
George Bush, of Texas, son of former president George
Bush. I thought to myself, "Man, does he ever look like his
father!" I had no trouble identifying whose son this guy is.

Identification carries with it at least two important
meanings. It refers to *likeness,* a trait of recognition and
similarity. In the Gospel of John, Jesus says, "If you really
knew me, you would know my Father as well" (14:7). A
little later in the same conversation, He says, "Anyone who
has seen me has seen the Father" (v. 9). Those are two pretty awesome statements.

When the Bible refers to the issue of holiness, it is basically a challenge for us to live in such a way that our attitudes and actions are becoming more and more like those
that reflect the nature and grace of God. What are those attitudes and actions? We can best discover them by a close
look at and personal encounter with Jesus Christ. "For
God, who said, 'Let light shine out of darkness,' made his
light shine in our hearts to give us the light of the knowledge of the glory of God *in the face of [Jesus] Christ*" (2 Corinthians 4:6, emphasis added).

So, identification means similarity. Christ becomes our
goal and measuring stick for godliness and a tremendous
example for each of us to pursue.

Identification also is about *wanting to be associated with
someone.* Educator and seminar speaker Howard Hendricks
tells the story of the time when his son was going through
a serious time of rebellion. His hair was long and stringy,
his style of dress was countercultural. One time he entered
a huge banquet hall in a sense of urgency to find his dad.
Howard describes his first reaction as he spotted his

mangy-looking son heading across the room toward him and his table full of important dinner companions.

"At first, I was embarrassed," Hendricks admitted. But God began to remind him, "This is your son. You may be embarrassed. But remember *you* have embarrassed *Me* plenty of times, and I still welcome you with open arms." By the time his son made it to the father's table, his dad was able to genuinely identify with his son by exclaiming to the whole table, "Hey, folks, this is my boy!"[1]

Jesus gives us a picture of the Father in heaven when He reminds us that He came for the sick and the sinners. He did not come to identify with respectable society or to help those with only a few small needs. "The Son of Man came to seek and to save what was lost" (Luke 19:10).

Identifying with someone is also about "walking in his or her shoes" for a while. Husbands and wives identify with each other when they trade roles and actually experience what each does and how it feels. Trying to put ourselves in the place of others is a wonderful way of identifying with them. The most effective way of developing grace and compassion is to find ways *before* we make judgments to put ourselves in the situation of another—actually or by imagination—to get the sense of how it must be physically, emotionally, spiritually. We can harshly criticize others for divorce only until we have a son or daughter who has suffered at the hands of a spouse. Then we become more understanding about why some folks make the decisions they do.

A dad who takes care of three kids for the week while Mom is on a trip begins to understand her exhaustion—even after fast-food breakfasts, lunches, and dinners. He begins to understand even without picking up the house each day, doing the laundry, buying the groceries, cleaning the house, paying the bills, listening to a husband gripe

---

1. The author heard Howard Hendricks tell this story.

about his poor treatment at work, fending off 20 telemarketing callers, and dealing with personal physical irritations.

God identifies with us about our lives here on earth. Really identifies. How? Through Jesus. The writer of the Book of Hebrews describes it this way: "We don't have a priest who is out of touch with our reality. [Jesus has] been through weakness and testing, experienced it all—all but the sin. So let's walk right up to him and get what he is so ready to give" (Hebrews 4:15, TM).

It is hard to put it any better than what Jesus says about persons who believe in Him. They do "not believe in me only, but in the one who sent me" (John 12:44). That is identification.

It is funny to watch children imitate an adult or other children playing with them. Those little winking, blinking games start young. They are a great way to know that the children are beginning to process some thoughts inside those new little brains and are sorting out ways of interacting with others.

Later in life we imitate those we admire. We talk like them, walk like them, and take on mannerisms of those individuals. At first, when the children are young and the imitations are innocent and fun, we laugh and think it is cute. Later in life, what our children imitate is not so much a game. The imitations can carry serious price tags, especially if they imitate our neglect of them because we are too busy making a living while they grow up.

A more mature and needed form of imitation is included in the word "mentoring." A mentor is one who is a role model and trainer for us. John 5:19-24 gives us a terrific look at the mentoring process from which we can learn and apply.

> Jesus gave them this answer: "I tell you the truth, the Son can do nothing by himself; he can do only what he sees his Father doing, because whatever the Father

does the Son also does. For the Father loves the Son and shows him all he does. Yes, to your amazement he will show him even greater things than these. For just as the Father raises the dead and gives them life, even so the Son gives life to whom he is pleased to give it. Moreover, the Father judges no one, but has entrusted all judgment to the Son, that all may honor the Son just as they honor the Father. He who does not honor the Son does not honor the Father, who sent him.

"I tell you the truth, whoever hears my word and believes him who sent me has eternal life and will not be condemned; he has crossed over from death to life."

God the Father is the Source. Just as a parent is the source for the life of a child, so is our Heavenly Father an original and ongoing Source for Jesus Christ—and the Source for each of us.

We are also reminded that God has shown to Jesus all He does. "The Son can do nothing by himself; he can do only what he sees his Father doing, because whatever the Father does the Son also does" (v. 19). In the same way, Jesus mentors us in life, love, and faith.

Children work to learn and accomplish that which their parents have trained them to do and to be. For example, how can we best teach children to safely cross a street? First, we take them with us and talk them through it. Then, we let them go with us and talk us through it. Then we let them do it while we watch. Eventually, they can safely do it on their own. Then at some point, the trainee becomes a mentor or trainer for another learner.

At some point, the Father passes the responsibility on to the Child. Jesus described this happening in verse 22, "The Father judges no one, but has entrusted all judgment to the Son." Then in John 17, Jesus describes "the passing of the torch" on to His disciples. And of course, that torch has been passed on to us nearly 2,000 years later.

One of the most direct statements in all the Bible about imitation is found in the words of Paul. "Be imitators of God, therefore, as dearly loved children and live a life of love, just as Christ loved us and gave himself up for us" (Ephesians 5:1-2).

Jesus puts a face on God for us. Not only that but a mind, a heart, and hands as well. The great Methodist missionary, Stanley Jones, says it this way, "The decisive difference between other religions and the gospel is that in other religions, their words became words. In Christ, the Word became flesh and camped out with us for a while."[2]

Religion is man's search for God. Christianity is about God's search for humanity. And the gospel calls on us to *want* to be found.

My wife and I have had great fun with our young grandchildren with our games of hide-and-seek, which we normally play down in our basement. Through this little game, I have learned more about what Jesus meant when He told us that He desired we become "like little children" (Matthew 18:3) if we would enter God's kingdom.

We take turns and work in teams for this hide-and-seek thing. We have to train the children how to play the game, because one part of it doesn't tend to come naturally. Let me explain.

I go upstairs and count. Then I come down the stairs, calling out in menacing tones, "Fee, fi, fo, fum. Here I come." I will look for them and talk out loud at the same time, saying, "You kids are really hiding well. I'm not sure I can find you."

About that time one of the younger and "less experienced" ones will call out, "Here I am! Here I am!" You see, little children *want* to be found.

The most magnificent truth that we can imagine and experience is the truth that God is so in love with each of

---

2. E. Stanley Jones, *The Word Became Flesh* (Nashville: Abingdon, 1963), 6.

us that He has gone to amazing extremes to get to know us and be known by us. This is the meaning and mission of Jesus Christ. God has come to visit us, to learn exactly what we face in life, and to express firsthand the extent of His love by dying for us in hopes of winning our love to Him. It is a great love story. In the process of all that, God is making a way for our sins to be forgiven without us having to pay eternal consequences, by taking the consequences for us through Jesus Christ's death by crucifixion.

Maybe the most profound statement in the Bible is John 1:14: "The Word [Jesus] became flesh and made his dwelling among us. We have seen his glory, the glory of the One and Only, who came from the Father, full of grace and truth."

God's great desire is to be known and loved by His creation—us. To help us do that, God entered His creation through Jesus Christ, got to know our needs personally, made a way to provide peace with himself for us, then invited us to accept His invitation.

Those of us who do respond to that invitation are invited to gladly identify with our Heavenly Father, desire to become like Him, and then invite Christ to live through us to make a difference in this world. What a deal!

Convicted bomber Timothy McVeigh had just been given the death sentence and evening news anchor Dan Rather was announcing the verdict. In a riveting moment of emotion, Rather quoted the prosecuting attorney as saying to the jury, "Ladies and gentlemen, you are looking," as he pointed to McVeigh, "into the face of a coward."

As Dan Rather read those words, his eyes were reddening and rapidly filling with tears. I wondered why. Was he angry at the thought of McVeigh? Newscasters usually hold their emotions in reserve. Then I think the reason became evident as I recalled that just before he quoted the prosecutor, a picture of McVeigh had been flashed across the screen with the announcement that standing beside him was William McVeigh, Timothy's father. Think of the feelings and thoughts of a father as he hears those things about his son. Yet there he was, still beside him. Why? "Because," he would probably say, "he is still my son."

Nearly 2,000 years ago, by a crowded baptism service in the Jordan River, a carpenter's son named Jesus was being baptized. However, the voice of His other Father boomed from the heavens with the words, "This is my Son, whom I love" (Matthew 3:17). We have seen the Son and are not disappointed, because He is just like His Father. And we are invited to join the family.

A Look at Ourselves

1. Name some ways in which you reflect your earthly parents' values and character.

2. Name some ways we can reflect our Heavenly Father's values and character.

3. What are some responses that help you to know whether someone thinks of Jesus as a "liar," a "lunatic," or the Lord?

4. What are one or two specific things you can do today that would reflect Christlike character?

About the author: David Holdren is senior pastor of Cypress Wesleyan Church in Galloway, Ohio.

CHAPTER 13

THE POWER BEHIND EVERYTHING

by Randy T. Hodges

A Look at the Characteristic
The Holy Spirit's power enabled Jesus.

A Look at Scripture
Luke 24:45-49; Acts 1:3-5

A Look at Jesus

Imagine Simon Peter's frustration toward the end of Jesus' time on earth: "I've spent three years following Jesus. I walked away from my work as a fisherman just to be near Him. I watched what He did when hurting people came for help. I saw how He responded when evil people tried to hurt Him. I've seen Jesus in good times and bad. And always He stayed centered in God, always He stayed in control, always He honored His Father. I want to be like Jesus.

"Long before the Crucifixion, I could see trouble coming. Jesus began to tell us that He would suffer, be rejected by the religious leaders, and even die. I couldn't stand to hear these thoughts, so I took Him aside, trying to tell Him not to talk so negatively. But Jesus told me to get away. I was tempting Him—tempting Him to reject God's plan for Him. He said I wasn't thinking like God at all. I wasn't very Christlike, was I?

"I've tried to be like Him, yet I mess up a lot. When they came to arrest Jesus, I wanted to defend Him. So, I whipped out my sword and took a swipe at the head of one of them. I got him too—sliced his ear right off. However, Jesus stepped in and stopped me. He lovingly reached out and replaced the ear of the one they call Malchus. I guess in my eagerness to defend Jesus I forgot all He taught us. I wasn't very Christlike, was I?

"I want to be like Jesus. But now, He's leaving. If I couldn't 'walk His walk' with Him here, how can I hope to be like Him after He's gone?"

It's easy to feel Peter's frustration. Many of us have struggled to be Christlike in a very unchristian world. When our help and support disappear, it's easy to be discouraged.

The Gospel of Luke and the Acts of the Apostles are both addressed to "Theophilus," which means "friend of God." This "friend of God" may have been a specific person that Luke wanted to tell of all God was doing, or it may have been a way of addressing his story to everyone whose heart the Holy Spirit is drawing to Jesus Christ— even you and me! Luke writes to provide a detailed and orderly history of all the exciting things God does for us in and through Jesus. He writes to help those who aren't yet Christians to come to Christ. Luke begins by telling the story of Jesus' life on earth. He continues the story in his second volume, Acts, by reporting those amazing events by which the Early Church turned their world upside down for God.

In the scripture passages cited at the beginning of this chapter we see three life-changing truths:

1. At the crucial moment, just before leaving for heaven, Jesus gave His followers final instructions.

When we have but a short time remaining together, we focus on what is most important. Jesus would soon return to heaven. The words Christ spoke in these crucial last moments came from deep within His heart. He concentrated, not on trivial side issues, but on what is most important. Jesus knew that His disciples needed to hear His closing challenge. He knows we still need to hear His words today.

2. Jesus focused on the gift His Father promised, the Holy Spirit's power, that His followers desperately need to live as Christians.

It's just like our Lord to focus, not on himself, but on the needs of those near Him. Part of being Christlike involves becoming centered, not in ourselves, but in God and the real needs of those around us. To the very end of His physical walk on earth, our Lord showed His concern to help those who follow Him.

3. This God-promised gift is given so Christ's work and ministry will continue.

All that Jesus accomplished while He was on earth was empowered by the Holy Spirit. The secret to Jesus' amazing life is revealed in Scripture: "Jesus returned to Galilee *in the power of the Spirit,* and news about him spread through the whole countryside" (Luke 4:14, emphasis added). No doubt, our Lord did many miraculous things—casting out evil spirits, healing the sick, even raising the dead. Yet, often He tried to downplay the miracles so people would not follow Him for the wrong reason. Still, because the Holy Spirit worked through Jesus, His life touched those around Him in powerful ways. His ministry made a difference.

Jesus entrusted the work to the followers He was leaving behind. So, He offered them the same divine power that energized His work and ministry—a power that would activate their witness for Christ. "You are witnesses of these things. I am going to send you what my Father has promised; but stay in the city until you have been clothed with power from on high" (Luke 24:48-49).

The power energizing Jesus' own ministry is the same

power He promised His disciples to invigorate their lives. This power would launch them forward. From the beginnings of ministry in Jerusalem to taking the gospel to the ends of the earth, the indwelling power of God would propel them forward.

A Look at Life

He told me, "I'm trying to live as a Christian, but I can't seem to do it by myself." It was obvious. This new follower of Christ was deeply frustrated in trying to live like Christ. To him, it seemed those Christians around him must have some secret strength. Or maybe they were just much stronger people who were better able to control themselves.

It wasn't that he had not come a long way. He had turned to Jesus months before. He had submitted to God when it became clear that his lifestyle was out of step with what God wanted from him. Still, certain things kept popping up, things that seemed especially tough to control. Overcoming long-entrenched habits that were rooted before he came to Christ was tough. Mastering a hot temper was even tougher.

"I'm trying to live as a Christian, but I can't seem to do it by myself." With struggles and tough battles like this ahead, how can new believers have any hope of successfully living a Christlike life?

How can weak and sometimes failing followers of Christ have any hope of effectively living a truly Christlike life? We need help—more power than we have in ourselves.

I once saw a marvelous photograph. A huge, Olympic-sized barbell with big, black plates weighing 500 pounds rests heavily on the ground. Behind the humongous weight stands a blond-haired little girl, just 18 months old, weighing at most 25 pounds. She sucks on a big, pink pacifier. Nevertheless, like a massive Olympic champion, she stands boldly behind the barbell, with both hands on the bar as if she is about to hoist the weight over her head. The great humor in this picture lies in the contrast—the massive weight versus the tiny girl without a chance of successfully raising the barbell.

A baby trying to hoist 500 pounds over her head is no less ridiculous than us attempting to successfully live like Christ by our own strength. We need help—more power than we have in ourselves. Christ shows us a better way, but living like Him sometimes seems impossible. It *is* impossible, unless we remember and employ the power that Christ promises His followers. He promises us all the power we need to live an effective Christlike life.

Christ promises power, but what kind of power? God offers power to be what He wants us to be—Christlike and holy.

One speaker has said, "Divine power is first of all moral power—power to be, more than power to do."[1] The enticing notion of power can quickly become a pursuit of the fantastic and spectacular. Yet, the life of Christ and the power He offers us is of another kind. It is first of all power to be—to be holy like our Lord himself. Spiritual power must remain tied to purity.

A former church leader wrote that the Spirit-filled believer's experience "differs from the life of a justified Christian in that it possesses inner power to walk before God in holiness and righteousness. It does not increase the burdens of the Christian life, but [it] does increase the power of the Christian experience. This is why sanctification is . . . 'regeneration made easy.'"[2]

God offers power to do what He calls us to do—to bear witness to Christ. We witness for Christ through *testi-*

---

1. Richard S. Taylor, "Holiness Preaching: Power," *Minister's Tape Club,* August 1984.
2. J. B. Chapman, *Holiness: The Heart of Christian Experience* (Albany, Oreg.: Sage Digital Library, 1996), 15.

mony. It takes courage to speak up for Christ, but we will not maintain courage apart from the indwelling power of the Holy Spirit. We witness for Christ through *service.* Becoming servants can drain us, but the indwelling Holy Spirit strengthens us and uses our service to touch other people, drawing them to Jesus Christ.

God offers us power to live the victorious Christian life . . .

> where He puts us—circumstances.
> with those around us—even the difficult people.
> for as long as He needs us—perseverance.
> with contentment, joy, and peace—attitude.

What kind of power does Christ promise? Another writer reminds us, "It is not abstract power . . . , but it is a Person, whose presence with you is necessary to your possessing and retaining the power. *He has the power, and you have Him.*"[3] The power we need and the power we can have is Christ Jesus living and working within us.

This leads us to examine ourselves and to ask an unavoidable question: Who can have the Spirit's power and how?

The truth is a marvelous one, for God is a marvelous God! God intends His power for *all believers.* Apart from the indwelling presence and power of the Holy Spirit, it is impossible for any Christian or church to ever live or work as God desires. God longs to provide you and me with this marvelous power—all the power we need to live a Christlike life.

Yet, God cannot trust His divine power to anyone with impure or selfish motives. The newspaper reported a horrible tragedy stemming from a seemingly innocent request. A 10-year-old asked his mom to move the family sedan so he could play basketball in the driveway. The 28-

---

3. A. B. Simpson, *Power from on High* (Harrisburg, Pa.: Christian Publications), 2:78.

year-old mother told her young son to back the car out of the driveway himself, and she went to watch. However, as the youngster shoved the car in gear, the vehicle veered out of control and backed over the mother, killing her in the process. What a horrible tragedy![4]

In giving the boy more power than he could handle, it destroyed the family's future together. Power can build, but power can also destroy.

Our requests for power seem innocent enough. We wonder why God doesn't give us more. Yet, God knows our hearts. He also knows that power apart from purity could be disastrous. Power must only be trusted to those able to handle it. So, He gives His power only to those with pure and love-filled hearts.

He gives His power only to those who fully surrender themselves to Him. Before God can trust us with His power, we must die to our desire for power. We get a glimpse of the problem of power-seeking in the person of Diotrephes (die-AH-trah-fees). John tells us Diotrephes "loves to be first" (3 John 9). This "church boss" busily used his position—his power—to get his own way, not to promote the work of Christ in the church. Ecclesiastical power of this kind is not at all the kind of power Jesus promised in the Holy Spirit.

One preacher observed that like Diotrephes, "the woods are full of persons who like to put themselves first. We may as well admit that perhaps the most common, and certainly the most devastating, manifestation of the carnal mind in the average church is the lust for power. . . . But the Holy Spirit's power will never rest upon us until we die out to being 'top dog' in the church."[5]

A different commentator wrote, "The filling of the Spirit takes away that restless ambition, that unseemly de-

---

4. Robert Short, *The Wichita Eagle,* May 24, 1997.
5. Taylor, "Holiness Preaching: Power."

sire for place and power and fame, and displaces it by a longing to be useful in service."[6] We must die to power before God can trust us with His power.

A Look at Ourselves

These questions may help us apply God's Word to our lives:

1. Do I long to be more Christlike in all I do?

2. Knowing Jesus saves me, have I offered myself to God, to serve Him any way He chooses? (Our complete consecration precedes the Spirit's filling our heart.)

3. Do I see in myself a likeness to my Lord, a likeness that shows itself in . . .

- a greater concern for those who don't know Jesus,
- a greater boldness in witnessing,
- a greater love for the people around me, and
- a greater evidence of the fruit of the Spirit in my life?

4. Do I access all of the Holy Spirit's power in every area of my life?

About the author: Dr. Randy Hodges is senior pastor of West Side Church of the Nazarene in Wichita, Kansas.

---

6. A. M. Hills, *Holiness and Power* (Albany, Oreg.: Sage Digital Library, 1996), 16.